CENTER FOR LANGUAGE
EDUCATION AND COOPERATION
教育部中外语言交流合作中心

天下一家

本书编写组 编

汉语桥

中文比赛备考有声读物

One World, One Family: Audio Book for "Chinese Bridge" Contestants

北京语言大学出版社
BEIJING LANGUAGE AND CULTURE
UNIVERSITY PRESS

图书在版编目（CIP）数据

天下一家 ："汉语桥"中文比赛备考有声读物 / 《天下一家 ："汉语桥"中文比赛备考有声读物》编写组编. -- 北京 ：北京语言大学出版社，2021.11
ISBN 978-7-5619-5889-6

Ⅰ. ①天…　Ⅱ. ①天…　Ⅲ. ①汉语－对外汉语教学－语言读物　Ⅳ. ①H195.5

中国版本图书馆 CIP 数据核字（2021）第 126095 号

天下一家——"汉语桥"中文比赛备考有声读物
TIANXIA YI JIA
——"HANYUQIAO" ZHONGWEN BISAI BEIKAO YOUSHENG DUWU

排版制作：北京创艺涵文化发展有限公司
责任印制：周　燚

出版发行：北京语言大学出版社
社　　址：北京市海淀区学院路 15 号，100083
网　　址：www.blcup.com
电子信箱：service@blcup.com
电　　话：编 辑 部　8610-82303647/3592/3395
　　　　　国内发行　8610-82303650/3591/3648
　　　　　海外发行　8610-82303365/3080/3668
　　　　　北语书店　8610-82303653
　　　　　网购咨询　8610-82303908
印　　刷：北京市金木堂数码科技有限公司

版　　次：2021 年 11 月第 1 版　　印　　次：2021 年 11 月第 1 次印刷
开　　本：710 毫米 × 1000 毫米　1/16　　印　　张：14
字　　数：200 千字
定　　价：100.00 元

PRINTED IN CHINA

天下一家——“汉语桥”中文比赛备考有声读物

总策划　马箭飞

策划　宋永波

主编　韩经太

副主编　张廷银　海　霞（录音）

执行副主编　滕连帅　丁利国　黄楷迪
王孝强　姜西良　李　搏（录音）

编者　汉　　语：王孝强　姜西良
英　　语：王秋生
法　　语：许　明
俄　　语：武保艳
西班牙语：刘　柳
阿拉伯语：周　行
日　　语：田　昊
朝 鲜 语：李　燕　蔡柯欣

中文审订　钱志熙　张　剑　周　亭　乐　琦　王学松　张　英

英文审订　吴　平

英文翻译　王秋生

录音统筹　葛　晓　李梦雨

录音后期　刘　宁　陈子严

中文录音　海　霞　苏　扬　滕　欢

英文录音　季小军　金利民　李纪萱　Thalia H

编写说明

“人类命运共同体”理念已经得到国际社会的高度认同。作为沟通中华文明与世界各国文明重要渠道的“汉语桥”，有必要进一步推广“天下一家”的国际共识。在有关方面的支持和领导下，北京语言大学师生编写了本读物。

读物从“命运与共”“和平相处”“睦邻友好”“文明互鉴”“包容互尊”“合作发展”六个方面来解读“天下一家”的概念并组织材料。在每个版块下，我们搜集、整理了相关名人名言和通行谚语（统称为“名句”），编成条目。

限于篇幅和时间，我们以国际通行的汉语、英语、法语、俄语、西班牙语和阿拉伯语六种语言为线索搜集相关资料，个别版块增加了日语和朝鲜语名句。各语种的排列顺序按照国际通行惯例；每一语种下的条目，按照出处或作者时代的先后排序。

每个条目原文下设有“译文”“作者及出处”“背景简介”“解析”四个部分。原文指该名句在其语种中的原始表述；“译文”指现代汉语翻译；“作者及出处”指名句的原作者或原出处；“背景简介”简要介绍该名句产生的基本背景；“解析”则围绕“天下一家”的基本理念，对该名句的意义稍作阐释。为便于阅读和理解，所有条目的“译文”“作者及出处”“背景简介”“解析”均以中英双语呈现（英语名句的“译文”部分只有现代汉语翻译）。

本读物的编写，得到了教育部中外语言交流合作中心和北京语言大学的关心、指导；参加编写的师生按照编写计划，反复论证，数易其稿；最后又请中华传统文化及中外文明交流方面的专家审稿把关。对有关机构和个人的热心支持及辛勤劳动，我们表示衷心感谢。因时间仓促，读物中难免存在讹误，祈请广大读者特别是外国读者朋友给予批评指正！

编写组

2021 年 11 月 2 日

目　录

第一部分　命运与共

第二部分　和平相处

第三部分　睦邻友好

第一部分

命运与共

一 汉语名句

1

各美其美，美人之美，美美与共，天下大同。

译文 Translated Text

人们既懂得欣赏自己创造的美，也懂得欣赏他人创造的美，不同的美和谐共存，这就是最理想的社会。

People appreciate not only the beauty created by themselves, but also that created by others. Different kinds of beauty coexist harmoniously and this is the most ideal society.

作者及出处 Author and Source

费孝通《人的研究在中国——个人的经历》。

Fei Xiaotong, “Anthropological Studies in China – My Personal Experience” .

背景简介 Background Knowledge

费孝通（1910—2005），中国著名社会活动家，中国社会学和人类学的奠基人之一。1988 年获联合国大英百科全书奖。

Fei Xiaotong (1910–2005), a famous Chinese social activist and one of the founders of Chinese sociology and anthropology, won the United Nations Encyclopædia Britannica Prize in 1988.

解析 Interpretation

费孝通提出了认识和处理不同文明之间关系的一种理想方式:“各美其美”是各个民族都有一套自身评价美的价值标准,“美人之美”是文化交流过程中逐渐形成的对其他民族的美的接纳,“美美与共”是对其他民族文化的进一步认同与文化间共同价值的建立,“天下大同”是人们所向往的美的最终境界。2014年6月28日,习近平主席在和平共处五项原则发表60周年纪念大会上的讲话中曾引用这句话。“天下大同”出自儒家经典《礼记 · 礼运》,用于描述社会和谐美好的状态。习近平借用这句话来说明不同文明之间可以在相互尊重、平等相待的基础上和谐相处,共同推动构建人类命运共同体。

Fei Xiaotong puts forward an ideal way to understand and deal with the relationship between different civilizations. “各美其美” means each nation has its own set of value standards to evaluate beauty. “美人之美” means in the process of cultural exchange, each nation gradually accepts the “beauty” of other nations. “美美与共” refers to the further recognition of the cultures of other nations and the establishment of common values among different cultures. “天下大同” is the ultimate state of “beauty” that people yearn for. On June 28, 2014, President Xi Jinping quoted these words at the commemorative ceremony marking the 60th anniversary of the release of the “Five Principles of Peaceful Coexistence” . “天下大同” is taken from the Confucian classic *The Book of Rites*, and is used to describe the harmonious and glorious state of society. Xi Jinping borrowed this sentence to show that different civilizations can live together harmoniously on the basis of mutual respect and equal treatment, and jointly promote the building of a community of shared future for mankind.

2

四海之内皆兄弟也。

译文 Translated Text

天下的人都亲如兄弟。

All the people within the four seas are brothers.

作者及出处 Author and Source

《论语·颜渊》。

The Analects (Book XII, Yan Yuan).

背景简介 Background Knowledge

《论语》是孔子弟子及再传弟子为记录孔子及其弟子言行而编成的语录集，较为集中地体现了孔子及儒家学派的政治主张、伦理思想、道德观念及教育原则。孔子（公元前551—公元前479），中国古代思想家、政治家、教育家，儒家学派创始人。

The Analects is a collection of quotations compiled by Confucius' disciples and his disciples' disciples to record the words and deeds of Confucius and his disciples. It embodies the political views, ethical thoughts, moral concepts and educational principles of Confucius and the Confucian School. Confucius (551 B.C.–479 B.C.) was an ancient Chinese thinker, statesman, educator, and founder of the Confucian School in the Spring and Autumn Period.

解析 Interpretation

“四海之内皆兄弟也”说的是天下的人都亲如手足兄弟。在中国人看来，既然是一家兄弟，就应该和睦相处，共同成长。同理，人类是一个命运共同体，世界各国也应该和平相处，合作共赢。2015 年 3 月 28 日，习近平主席在博鳌亚洲论坛 2015 年年会上的主旨演讲中曾引用此语，并指出：“中华民族历来爱好和平，自古就崇尚‘以和为贵’‘协和万邦’‘四海之内皆兄弟也’等思想。”“中国将毫不动摇坚持独立自主的和平外交政策，坚持走和平发展道路，坚持互利共赢的开放战略，秉持正确义利观，推动建立以合作共赢为核心的新型国际关系，始终做维护世界和平、促进共同发展的坚定力量。”

This sentence means that people all over the world are intimate like brothers. In the eyes of the Chinese people, since we are brothers in the same family, we are supposed to live in harmony and grow up together. Similarly, all mankind is a community of shared future, and all countries in the world should live in peace through win-win cooperation. On March 28, 2015, in the keynote speech delivered at the Boao Forum for Asia annual conference, President Xi Jinping quoted the sentence and pointed out that “the Chinese nation loves peace and has, since ancient times, held high such philosophies that ‘harmony is the most valuable’, ‘peace and harmony should prevail’ and ‘all the people within the four seas are brothers’.” “China will be steadfast in pursuing the independent foreign policy of peace, the path of peaceful development, the win-win strategy of opening-up, and the approach of upholding justice while pursuing shared interests. China will work to promote a new type of international relations of win-win cooperation and will always remain a staunch force for world peace and common development.”

3

仁者，以天地万物为一体。

译文 Translated Text

仁者认为天地万物与自己是浑然一体的。

Benevolent people think that they are integrated with everything in the world.

作者及出处 Author and Source

程颢、程颐《二程遗书·二先生语二上》。

Cheng Hao and Cheng Yi, *Quotations from Cheng Hao and Cheng Yi* (Vol. II, Part I).

背景简介 Background Knowledge

程颢（1032—1085），北宋哲学家、教育家、诗人，宋代理学的奠基者。程颐（1033—1107），北宋哲学家、思想家，宋代理学的创立人之一。

Cheng Hao (1032–1085) was a philosopher, educator, poet and founder of Neo-Confucianism in the Northern Song Dynasty. Cheng Yi (1033–1107) was a philosopher, thinker and one of the founders of Neo-Confucianism in the Northern Song Dynasty.

解析 Interpretation

在中国传统文化中，“仁”是儒家哲学的核心概念，“以天地万物为一体”是仁者追求的至高境界。2016 年 11 月 21 日，习近平主席在秘鲁国会发表的演讲中曾引用此语来阐释中国的一贯主张：“世界各国共同努力，建立平等相待、互商互谅的伙伴关系，公道正义、共建共享的安全格局，开放创新、包容互惠的发展前景，和而不同、兼收并蓄的文明交流，尊崇自然、绿色发展的生态体系。”中国人历来讲仁爱、尚和合，习近平借此呼吁各国要推动构建以合作共赢为核心的新型国际关系，构建人类命运共同体。

In Chinese traditional culture, “benevolence” is the core concept of Confucian philosophy, and “the integration of people and everything in the world” is the highest goal pursued by benevolent people. In the speech delivered by President Xi Jinping, at the Peruvian Congress on November 21, 2016, he quoted this sentence to explain China's consistent view, that is, “all countries in the world should make joint efforts to establish a partnership featuring equal treatment, consultation and mutual accommodation, a shared security pattern featuring fairness, justice and joint construction, a development prospect of openness, innovation, inclusiveness and reciprocity, cultural exchanges featuring harmony in diversity and open mind, and an ecosystem with respect for nature and green development.” The Chinese people have always emphasized benevolence and harmony. Xi Jinping called on all countries to promote the construction of a new type of international relations with win-win cooperation as its core and build a community of shared future for mankind.

4

民胞物与。

译文 Translated Text

每个人都是我的同胞，世间万物都是我的同类。

Everyone is my compatriot, and everything in the world is of the same kind as me.

作者及出处 Author and Source

张载《正蒙·乾称篇》。

Zhang Zai, *Correcting Youthful Ignorance* (Chapter XVII, Heavenly Designations).

背景简介 Background Knowledge

张载（1020—1077），北宋思想家、教育家，理学创始人之一。张载的原话是“民吾同胞，物吾与也”，后世常用为四字成语“民胞物与”。

Zhang Zai (1020–1077) was a thinker, educator and one of the founders of Neo-Confucianism in the Northern Song Dynasty. His original sentence is “民吾同胞，物吾与也” and is shortened to “民胞物与” by later generations.

解析 Interpretation

“民胞物与”的哲学基础是儒家“万物一体”“天人合一”的思想。在张载看来，每个人都是他的同胞，世间万物都是他的同类。全人类是一个命运共同体，作为生命个体，应该尽自己的伦理责任和道德义务，关爱社会上生存状态各异的族群，同时要秉持人与自然共生共存的理念，不应为了自身的生存而无限度地征服自然。“民胞物与”是中国古代的思想精华。2017年12月1日，习近平总书记在中国共产党与世界政党高层对话会上的主旨讲话中曾说：“中华民族历来讲求‘天下一家’，主张民胞物与、协和万邦、天下大同，憧憬‘大道之行，天下为公’的美好世界。”

The philosophical basis of the sentence is the Confucian thought of “the unity of all things” and “the unity of heaven and man” . In Zhang Zai’s opinion, everyone is his compatriot, and everything in the world is of the same kind as him. All human beings are a community of shared future. As individuals, they should shoulder their ethical responsibilities and moral obligations, care for ethnic groups with different living conditions in the society, and uphold the concept of coexistence between man and nature, but they should not exploit nature indefinitely for their own survival. “民胞物与” is the essence of Chinese ancient ideological thoughts. On December 1, 2017, Xi Jinping, General Secretary of the CPC Central Committee, said at the CPC in Dialogue with

World Political Parties High-Level Meeting, “The Chinese nation has always been stressing that ‘all people under heaven are of one family’ , advocating the views that ‘everyone is my compatriot, and everything in the world is of the same kind as me’ , ‘peace and harmony should prevail’ , ‘great harmony is expected in the world’ , and longing for the bright prospect of ‘the whole world as one community’ .”

5

四海之内若一家。

译文 Translated Text

天下就像一家人一样。

The whole world is like one family.

作者及出处 Author and Source

荀子《荀子·儒效》。

Xun Zi, *Xun Zi* (Chapter VIII, The Effects of Confucianism).

背景简介 Background Knowledge

荀子（约公元前313—公元前238），战国末期思想家、文学家、政治家。

Xun Zi (c. 313 B.C.–238 B.C.) was a famous thinker, writer and politician at the end of the Warring States Period.

解析 Interpretation

"四海之内若一家"，就是说天下如同一家。由于天赋秉性、兴趣爱好等各有不同，一家人有时难免会有不同的意见和行为，但始终都有共同的目标和一致的理想追求，那就是全家人共同的幸福生活。人类也是如此。2017 年 12 月 1 日，习近平总书记在中国共产党与世界政党高层对话会上的主旨讲话中指出：“世界各国尽管有这样那样的分歧矛盾，也免不了产生这样那样的磕磕碰碰，但世界各国人民都生活在同一片蓝天下、拥有同一个家园，应该是一家人。世界各国人民应该秉持‘天下一家’理念，张开怀抱，彼此理解，求同存异，共同为构建人类命运共同体而努力。”宇宙只有一个地球，人类共有一个家园。构建人类命运共同体，需要世界各国民众开放心态，普遍参与，共同努力。

In a family, because of the difference in talent, temperament, interests and hobbies of the family members, sometimes it's hard to avoid different opinions and behaviors. However, they always have the same goal and the same pursuit of the ideal, that is, the happy life of the whole family. The same is true with the whole human race. On December 1, 2017, Xi Jinping, General Secretary of the CPC Central Committee, said at the CPC in Dialogue with World Political Parties High-Level Meeting, “Although there are various differences and contradictions, as well as various inevitable collisions, between different countries, the people of all countries in the world live under the same blue sky and have the same home, so they should be of one family. People all over the world should uphold the concept of ‘all people under heaven are of one family’ , open their arms, understand each other, seek common ground while reserving differences, and work together to build a community of shared future for mankind." There is only one earth in the universe, and human beings share one home. To build a community with a shared future for mankind, people all over the world need to be broad-minded, participate universally and work concertedly.

6

大道之行也，天下为公。

译文 Translated Text

当最高理想实现的时候，天下将为人们所共有。

When the loftiest ideal is realized, the world will be shared by all people.

作者及出处 Author and Source

《礼记·礼运》。

The Book of Rites (Chapter IX, The Conveyance of Rites).

背景简介 Background Knowledge

《礼记》是中国古代重要的典章制度选集，相传为西汉学者、礼学家戴圣编纂，主要记载先秦的礼制，体现了先秦儒家的哲学思想、教育思想、政治思想、美学思想，是研究先秦社会和儒家思想的重要资料。

The Book of Rites is an important anthology of ancient Chinese laws and regulations, purportedly compiled by the Western Han scholar and expert of Confucian ritual Dai Sheng. It mainly records the rites of the pre-Qin period, embodies the philosophy, education, politics and aesthetics of the pre-Qin Confucianism, and is an important material for the study of the pre-Qin society and Confucianism.

解析 Interpretation

“大道之行也，天下为公”展现的是中国人心目中最理想、最美好的社会愿景，也就是中国人常说的大同世界的社会图景。“大道之行也，天下为公”是在终极理想的层面，期望能够化天下为一家，化四海为兄弟，使整个世界成为一个休戚与共的共同体。

This sentence shows the most ideal and beautiful social vision in the eyes of the Chinese people, that is, the social prospect of the world of great harmony that the Chinese people often talk about. “When the loftiest ideal is realized, the world will be shared by all people” is a hope at the level of the ultimate ideal that the world will be turned into one big family and all the people within the four seas will be brothers, so that the whole world will become a community of shared future, which shares weal and woe.

7

老吾老，以及人之老；幼吾幼，以及人之幼。

译文 Translated Text

尊敬自己的老人，并把这种尊敬推及别人的老人；爱护自己的孩子，并把这种爱护推及别人的孩子。

Extend the respect for the aged in one's own family to those of other families; extend the love for the children in one's own family to those of other families.

作者及出处 Author and Source

孟子《孟子·梁惠王上》。

Mencius, *Mencius* (King Hui of Liang, Part I).

背景简介 Background Knowledge

孟子（约公元前372—公元前289），战国时期的哲学家、思想家、政治家、教育家，是孔子之后儒家学派的代表人物，与孔子并称“孔孟”。

Mencius (c. 372 B.C.–289 B.C.) was a philosopher, thinker, statesman and educator in the Warring States Period. He was the representative of the Confucian School after Confucius, and is referred to as “Confucius and Mencius” together with Confucius.

解析 Interpretation

这句话是孟子关于家庭伦理和理想社会的重要名言。“老吾老，以及人之老”中有三个“老”字，第一个“老”是动词，意为“赡养”“尊敬”，后面两个“老”是名词，意指“老人”“长辈”。“幼吾幼，以及人之幼”中有三个“幼”字，第一个“幼”意为“抚养”“爱护”，后面两个“幼”都指“子女”“后辈”。在孟子之前，儒家经典《礼记·礼运》在描绘大同世界时说：“故人不独亲其亲，不独子其子，使老有所终，壮有所用，幼有所长，矜、寡、孤、独、废疾者皆有所养。”孟子继承了这种思想，用“老吾老，以及人之老；幼吾幼，以及人之幼”这句话来描述他心目中的理想社会图景，体现出他对家庭伦理的重视和对大同世界的追求。

This is an important saying that embodies Mencius' family ethics and his prospect of the ideal society. In the sentence “老吾老，以及人之老”, there are three words of “老”. The first “老” is a verb, which means “support” or “respect”; the second and third “老” are both nouns, meaning “the aged” or “the elders”. Likewise, in the sentence “幼吾幼，以及人之幼”, there are three words of “幼”. The first “幼” is a verb, which means “support” or “love”; the second and third “幼” are both nouns, meaning “children” or “the younger generation”. In both sentences, the word “及” has the meaning of “extend”. Before Mencius, while describing the world of great harmony, the

Confucian classic *The Book of Rites* said: “So we cannot only support our own parents, nor only nurture our own children, and we should ensure that the elderly can live their full lifespan, the middle-aged can serve the society, the young can grow up smoothly, and the widowed, the orphans, the childless as well as the disabled can all be supported.” Mencius inherited this thought, and described his ideal social prospect with the remark “Extend the respect for the aged in one’s own family to those of other families; extend the love for the children in one’s own family to those of other families” , which reflects his emphasis on family ethics and his pursuit of the world of great harmony.

二 英语名句

8

No man is an island, entire of itself.

译文 Translated Text

没有人是一座孤岛，可以自全。

作者及出处 Author and Source

约翰·邓恩的诗歌《没有人是一座孤岛》。

John Donne, the poem "No Man Is an Island" .

背景简介 Background Knowledge

约翰·邓恩（1572—1631），英国玄学派诗人。

John Donne (1572–1631) was a British metaphysical poet.

解析 Interpretation

在《没有人是一座孤岛》（1624）这首诗中，诗人讲述了整体和部分的密切关系，他认为没有人能像孤岛一样，可以独善其身。他把每个人比作大陆的一片，都是整体的一部分。如果缺少某一部分，整体固有的和谐就会被破坏。

In the poem "No Man Is an Island" (1624), the poet talks about the close relationship between the whole and the part. He believes that no one can make himself complete like an island. He compares everyone to a piece of the land, a part of the whole. If a part is missing, the inherent harmony of the whole will be destroyed.

9

All are needed by each one;
Nothing is fair or good alone.

译文 Translated Text

世间万物相互依存；
任何美好事物皆不单独存在。

作者及出处 Author and Source

拉尔夫·沃尔多·爱默生的诗歌《个体与整体》。

Ralph Waldo Emerson, the poem “Each and All” .

背景简介 Background Knowledge

拉尔夫·沃尔多·爱默生（1803—1882），美国哲学家、散文家、诗人，美国超验主义的主要代表人物。

Ralph Waldo Emerson (1803–1882) was an American philosopher, essayist, poet, and the main spokesman of American Transcendentalism.

解析 Interpretation

《个体与整体》的灵感源于爱默生1834年写的一篇日记。爱默生试图在这首诗歌中捕捉美的概念，他认为美是一种世间万物相互依存的状态，事物之间的命运有着内在的联系，不可分割。

The selected lines are taken from Emerson's poem "Each and All" , which gains its inspiration from a journal he worte in 1834. In this poem, Emerson endeavors to capture the concept of beauty, which he believes is a state of interdependence among all things in the world, whose fates are intrinsically linked and inseparable.

10

When peace has been broken anywhere, the peace of all countries everywhere is in danger.

译文 Translated Text

任何地方的和平一旦被打破，所有国家的和平亦将处于危险之中。

作者及出处 Author and Source

富兰克林·德兰诺·罗斯福，选自乔斯林·潘所编的《美国总统的聪明才智：语录》。

Franklin Delano Roosevelt, from *Wit and Wisdom of the American Presidents: A Book of Quotations.* Ed. Joslyn Pine.

背景简介 Background Knowledge

富兰克林·德兰诺·罗斯福（1882—1945），美国第32任总统，美国历史上首位连任4届的总统，曾多次被评为美国最佳总统，被《大西洋月刊》评为影响美国的100位人物之第4名。

Franklin Delano Roosevelt (1882–1945) was the 32nd President of the United States. He was the first president in American history to serve four consecutive terms. He was repeatedly named the best president of the United States and ranked the 4th of the 100 most influential people in American history by *The Atlantic*.

解析 Interpretation

在反法西斯战争的背景下，1939 年 9 月 3 日，英法对德宣战数小时后，罗斯福总统通过“炉边谈话”的形式发表了演讲，这句话就出自此次演讲。通过对战争形势的密切关注，罗斯福总统认为任何地区的和平与否都将影响整个世界，国与国之间是息息相关、命运与共的。

This line is from a speech President Roosevelt gave in the form of a “fireside chat” on September 3, 1939 during the Second World War, just hours after Britain and France declared war on Germany. Out of close analysis of the war scenario, he believed that the peace of anywhere would affect the whole world, and that all countries were closely related to each other and shared the common destiny.

11

All the nations and peoples are too closely knit together today for any one of them to imagine that it can live apart. Peace has been said to be indivisible, so is freedom, so is prosperity now, and so also is disaster in this one world that can no longer be split into isolated fragments.

译文 Translated Text

当今世界，所有的国家和民族都十分紧密地联系在一起，因此，任何一个国家和民族都无法想象自己可以离群索居。和平是不可分割的，自由是如此，繁荣亦是如此；同样，在这个不可再支离破碎的世界上，灾难也是不可分割的。

作者及出处 Author and Source

贾瓦哈拉尔·尼赫鲁，1947 年 8 月 14 日在新德里的制宪会议上名为《与命运之约》的演讲。

Jawaharlal Nehru, from the speech “A Tryst with Destiny” to the Constituent Assembly in New Delhi on August 14, 1947.

背景简介 Background Knowledge

贾瓦哈拉尔·尼赫鲁（1889—1964），印度政治家、革命家，印度开国总理。

Jawaharlal Nehru (1889–1964) was an Indian statesman and revolutionary, and was the founding prime minister of India.

解析 Interpretation

尼赫鲁这句话表示，全世界各个国家和各个民族之间都是紧密相连、不可分割的，各个国家和各个民族之间同甘苦、共患难，命运息息相关。这句话很好地解释了人类命运共同体的含义，体现了命运与共的主题。

The quote from Nehru means that all the countries and nations of the world are correlated and indivisible. They share weal and woe, and their destinies are closely linked. This quote well expresses the meaning of building a community with a shared future for mankind and reflects the theme of common destiny.

12

I feel we are all islands – in a common sea.

译文 Translated Text

我感觉，我们都是岛屿，共处同一片海洋。

作者及出处 Author and Source

安妮·莫罗·林德伯格《大海的礼物》。

Anne Morrow Lindbergh, *Gift from the Sea*.

背景简介 Background Knowledge

安妮·莫罗·林德伯格（1906—2001），美国女飞行员、作家。

Anne Morrow Lindbergh (1906–2001) was an American female pilot and writer.

解析 Interpretation

散文集《大海的礼物》充满了作者的人生经验和哲学沉思，曾一度位居美国畅销书榜首。在这本书中，作者思考了个体与整体的关系，认为虽然人人都是独立的个体，但在精神上却是彼此联系、彼此需要的。人类命运与共，就像岛屿一样，相连于同一片大海，同时又保持着独立完整、互不侵犯、互不干扰的状态，共同维护着世界的和谐美好。

Anne's collection of essays, *Gift from the Sea*, once a top American bestseller, is full of her life experience and philosophical contemplation. In this book, she reflects on the relationship between the individual and the whole, arguing that all people are independent individuals, but are spiritually connected and in need of each other. Human beings share a common destiny, similar to islands connected by a common sea. Meanwhile we remain independent and intact, non-intrusive and non-interfering, together maintaining the harmony and beauty of the world.

13

Our challenge is to remind ourselves of our common interests, our common ground, and to remind ourselves of our common dreams.

译文 Translated Text

我们面临的挑战是要提醒自己我们有着共同的利益、共同的立场，也要提醒自己我们有着共同的梦想。

作者及出处 Author and Source

珍妮特·雷诺，1997 年 1 月 15 日作为美国司法部部长的讲话。

Janet Reno, Speech of United States Attorney General, on January 15, 1997.

背景简介 Background Knowledge

珍妮特·雷诺（1938—2016），美国第一位女司法部部长，20 世纪美国任期最长的司法部部长。

Janet Reno (1938–2016) was the first female Attorney General in the United States and the longest-serving Attorney General of the 20th century in the United States.

解析 Interpretation

珍妮特·雷诺赞扬了人权运动蕴含的不屈精神和人权运动者们为实现公平公正做出的不懈努力。她号召各民族、各种族放下偏见，打破桎梏，和睦共处，共同创造一个自由、平等、正义的世界。

Janet Reno praises the unyielding spirit of the human rights movement and the unremitting efforts of human rights activists to strive for fairness and justness. She calls on all nations and all races to put aside their prejudices, break the shackles and live together in harmony to create a world of freedom, equality and justice.

14

More than ever before in human history, we share a common destiny. We can master it only if we face it together.

译文 Translated Text

人类历史上从来没有一刻像现在这样，我们同呼吸、共命运。我们只有共同面对才能掌控命运。

作者及出处 Author and Source

科菲·安南，转引自安德鲁·海伍德所著的《全球政治》。

Kofi Annan, from *Global Politics* by Andrew Heywood.

背景简介 Background Knowledge

科菲·安南（1938—2018），加纳外交官，联合国第七任秘书长，2001 年诺贝尔和平奖获得者。

Kofi Annan (1938–2018) was a Ghanaian diplomat who once served as the seventh Secretary-General of the United Nations. He won the Nobel Peace Prize in 2001.

解析 Interpretation

在 1999 年 12 月 15 日的联合国大会上，安南发表了题为《新千年的信息》的演讲，指出当今世界全球化趋势不可阻挡，全人类的命运紧密联系在一起，人类只有共同面对才能渡过种种难关。

At the United Nations General Assembly on December 15, 1999, Annan delivered the speech entitled "Message for the New Millennium" , in which he pointed out that the trend of globalization was inevitable and the destiny of mankind was closely related in today's world; only through facing the difficulties together, could we overcome them.

15

I hope that people will finally come to realize that there is only one "race" – the human race – and that we are all members of it.

译文 Translated Text

我希望人们最终会认识到世界上只有一个"种族"——人类，而我们都是这个"种族"的一员。

作者及出处 Author and Source

玛格丽特·阿特伍德，转引自丹尼尔·怀特三世所著的《致黑人年轻人的信》。

Margaret Atwood, from *Mo' Letters to Young Black Men* by Daniel Whyte III.

背景简介 Background Knowledge

玛格丽特·阿特伍德，生于 1939 年，加拿大小说家、诗人、文学评论家。

Margaret Atwood (born in 1939) is a Canadian novelist, poet and literary critic.

解析 Interpretation

玛格丽特·阿特伍德这句话表明，全世界人类的身份都是相同的，我们都是世界这个整体的一部分，我们命运相连、休戚与共。这句话表达了她种族平等的思想，反映了人类命运与共的主题。

The quote from Margaret Atwood means that human identity is the same all over the world, and that we are all parts of a whole, sharing weal and woe. This quote expresses her idea of racial equality and reflects the theme of mankind sharing a common destiny.

三
法语名句

16

Tout le genre humain n’est qu’une famille dispersée sur la face de toute la terre.

译文 **Translated Text**

人类是散布全球的一家人。

Human beings are a family spreading all over the world.

作者及出处 **Author and Source**

弗朗索瓦·费纳隆《忒勒马科斯历险记》。

François Fénelon, *The Adventures of Telemachus*.

背景简介 **Background Knowledge**

弗朗索瓦·费纳隆（1651—1715），法国神学家、教育家、作家，18 世纪启蒙运动的先驱之一。

François Fénelon (1651–1715) was a French theologian, educator, writer, and one of the pioneers of the Enlightenment in the 18th century.

解析 Interpretation

费纳隆认为所有人都是兄弟，人们应当像兄弟一样互相关爱。在《忒勒马科斯历险记》这部作品中，和平是费纳隆反复强调的主题，战争被形容为“人类的耻辱”。在这句名言中，作者认为全人类都是一家人，地球是我们共同的家园，只有视天下人为一家，大家才能够和睦相处。

Fénelon believes that all men are brothers and that people should love each other like brothers. In *The Adventures of Telemachus*, war is described as “the shame of mankind” . Peace is the theme repeatedly emphasized by Fénelon in this book. In this famous quote, the author thinks that all human beings are of one family and the earth is our common home, and only by regarding all people in the world as one family, can all people live together harmoniously.

17

Un jour, espérons-le, le globe entier sera civilisé, tous les points de la demeure humaine seront éclairés, et alors sera accompli le magnifique rêve de l'intelligence : avoir pour patrie le Monde et pour nation l'Humanité.

译文 Translated Text

终有一天，全球都会变成文明的世界，人类存在的每一个角落都将被照亮，人类智慧的宏伟梦想也终将实现：以世界为家园，视全人类为同一民族。

Sooner or later, the world will become a civilized world, every corner of the world where human beings exist will be illuminated, and the great dream of human wisdom will be realized as well, that is, taking the world as our home, and the whole human race as one nation.

作者及出处 Author and Source

维克多·雨果《老顽固》。

Victor Hugo, *Les Burgraves*.

背景简介 Background Knowledge

维克多·雨果（1802—1885），法国浪漫主义作家、诗人，其作品中蕴含着浓厚的博爱和人道主义思想。

Victor Hugo (1802–1885) was a French romantic writer and poet, whose works contain a strong sense of fraternity and humanitarianism.

解析 Interpretation

作为人道主义者，雨果没有狭隘的民族主义情绪，而是站在全人类的角度赞扬世界文明。雨果希望人与人之间友爱相处、和谐共存，而不是始终处于暴力对抗的状态，这也正是他的作品所表达的价值追求。

As a humanist, Hugo did not have narrow nationalist stances, but praised the world civilization from the perspective of all mankind. Hugo hoped that people could get along with each other in a friendly and harmonious way, rather than being always in a situation of violent antagonism, and this is also the value he pursued in his works.

18

Le bien-être de la partie signifie le bien-être du tout et la misère des uns apporte la misère de tous.

译文 Translated Text

部分人的幸福意味着所有人的幸福，部分人的痛苦承载着所有人的痛苦。

The happiness of some people means the happiness of all people, and the pain of some people bears the weight of the pain of all people.

作者及出处 Author and Source

守基·埃芬迪《致国民》。

Shoghi Effendi, *Call to the Nations*.

背景简介 Background Knowledge

守基·埃芬迪（1897—1957），巴哈伊信仰的核心人物阿博都·巴哈的长外孙。他个人有一些著作，内容主要涉及对信仰核心人物著作的解释与对信仰未来的指引。

Shoghi Effendi (1897–1957) was the eldest grandson of

'Abdu' l-Bahá who was the core figure of Bahá' í Faith. He wrote some works which mainly involve the interpretation of the works of the core figures of Bahá' í Faith and the guidance of its future.

解析 Interpretation

在《致国民》中，守基·埃芬迪提到，世界正在走向自己的命运。世界各国人民和各民族之间相互依存，无论那些制造分裂的人说什么或做什么，这已经是一个事实。而正因为如此，部分人的幸福意味着所有人的幸福，部分人的痛苦意味着所有人的痛苦。

In *Call to the Nations*, Shoghi Effendi mentions that the world is moving towards its own destiny. It is an established fact that all the people and nations of the world depend on each other, no matter what those who provoke divisions say or do. Just because of this, the happiness of some people means the happiness of all people, and the pain of some people means the pain of all people.

19

Nous avons besoin les uns des autres. L’être humain n’est pas fait pour s’isoler, mais pour partager.

译文 Translated Text

人类彼此依赖。人因共享而生，而非孤立存在。

Human beings depend on each other. People are born to share, not to exist in isolation.

作者及出处 Author and Source

爱丽丝·帕里索。

Alice Pariso.

背景简介 Background Knowledge

爱丽丝·帕里索（1930—1990），加拿大作家。

Alice Pariso (1930–1990) was a Canadian writer.

解析 Interpretation

作者认为人类是彼此依赖而生存的，所以人与人之间应该和睦相处。

The author thinks that human beings depend on each other for existence, and therefore people should live in harmony.

20

L’unité de l’humanité signifie : personne ne peut s’échapper nulle part.

译文 Translated Text

人类的一体性表明，没有人可以孤立存在。

The unity of human beings shows that no one can exist in isolation.

作者及出处 Author and Source

米兰·昆德拉《小说的艺术》。

Milan Kundera, *The Art of the Novel*.

背景简介 Background Knowledge

米兰·昆德拉，小说家，1929 年出生于捷克斯洛伐克的布尔诺，自 1975 年起在法国定居。《小说的艺术》是米兰·昆德拉关于他写作观念的文学批评著作。

Milan Kundera (born in 1929) is a novelist born in Brno, Czechoslovakia, and has settled in France since 1975. Based on his own experience, *The Art of the Novel* is Kundera’s work of literary criticism illustrating his view on writing.

解析 Interpretation

这句话表达了人的社会性和一体性。作者用了“unité de l'humanité”这个短语，传达出“天下一家”的观念。

This quote expresses the sociality and unity of human beings. The author uses the phrase “unité de l'humanité” to express the concept of “all people under heaven are of one family” .

21

Le monde du partage devra remplacer le partage du monde.

译文 Translated Text

共享的世界必将取代分裂的世界。

The world of sharing is bound to replace the world of division.

作者及出处 Author and Source

克劳德·勒鲁什《雄狮萨姆》(*Itinéraire d'un enfant très gâté*)。

Claude Lelouch, *Itinerary of a Very Spoiled Child*.

背景简介 Background Knowledge

克劳德·勒鲁什，生于 1937 年，法国导演、编剧、制片人、摄影师、演员。

Claude Lelouch (born in 1937) is a French director, screenwriter, producer, photographer, and actor.

解析 Interpretation

这句话出自《雄狮萨姆》这本书，《雄狮萨姆》也是克劳德·

勒鲁什导演的电影。作者认为世界应当是人们共享的，是同甘共苦的，而不应当是四分五裂的。

This quote comes from Claude Lelouch's autobiography *Itinéraire d'un enfant très gâté* (*Itinerary of a Very Spoiled Child*). Lelouch has directed a similarly titled film. This quote means that the world should be a shared one, with people sharing weal and woe, instead of a split and disunited one.

四 俄语名句

22

Дружба пяти континентов – гарантия мира в веках.

译文 Translated Text

五大洲的友谊是永久和平的保障。

Friendship among the five continents is the guarantee of peace forever.

作者及出处 Author and Source

俄罗斯克拉斯诺亚尔斯克市纪念碑上的箴言。

A motto carved on a monument in Krasnoyarsk, Russia.

背景简介 Background Knowledge

此箴言虽流传于苏联时期，但对当今世界仍具有重要的现实意义。

This motto was widespread in the Soviet Union, but it still has important practical significance to the world today.

解析 Interpretation

五大洲各国人民不分种族、肤色、年龄，无论过去、现在和未来，都应坚守世界的和平与稳定。在人类友好交往的历史长河中，各国人民相互联通、相互依存的程度逐步加深，形成了你中有我、我中有你的人类命运共同体。各国一道维护世界和平，才能促进共同发展。

The people in the five continents, regardless of their race, skin color or age, should firmly defend world peace and stability no matter in the past, at present or in the future. In the long history of friendly human exchanges, the degree of mutual connection and interdependence of all countries has gradually deepened, forming a community of shared future for mankind. All countries should work together to maintain world peace and promote common development.

五 阿拉伯语名句

23

أحببت نفسي. ثم أحببت وطني مصر. ثم أحببت قومي العرب، ثم أحببت الإنسانية جمعاء.

译文 Translated Text

我爱自己，我爱我的祖国埃及，我爱阿拉伯民族，我爱全人类。

I love myself, love my motherland Egypt, love the Arab nations, and love all mankind.

作者及出处 Author and Source

阿卜杜·拉扎克·桑胡里（عبد الرزاق السنهوري）。

Abd El-Razzak El-Sanhuri.

背景简介 Background Knowledge

阿卜杜·拉扎克·桑胡里（1895—1971），埃及法学家。他不仅为阿拉伯法律奠定了基础，还为后世留下了诸多名言警句。

Abd El-Razzak El-Sanhuri (1895–1971) was a famous Egyptian jurist. He not only laid the foundation of Arabian law, but also left many famous aphorisms for later generations.

解析 Interpretation

这句话强调从自爱出发，将爱扩展到祖国、阿拉伯世界，乃至全世界、全人类。全人类本是一个命运共同体，所以应该用爱来联结并巩固它。

This quote stresses that love should start from the love of oneself, and then be extended to the motherland, the Arab world and finally the whole world and all mankind. Mankind is a community of shared future, so it should be connected and strengthened with love.

24

فالأرض كلها وطني، والعائلة البشرية عشيرتي.

译文 Translated Text

地球皆吾国，他家亦吾亲。

The earth is my country, and the human family is my clan.

作者及出处 Author and Source

纪·哈·纪伯伦（جبران خليل جبران）《泪与笑》。

Gibran Kahlil Gibran, *A Tear and a Smile*.

背景简介 Background Knowledge

纪·哈·纪伯伦（1883—1931），黎巴嫩作家、诗人、画家，阿拉伯文学的主要奠基人，20 世纪阿拉伯新文学道路的开拓者之一。

Gibran Kahlil Gibran (1883–1931) was a writer, poet and painter of Lebanon. He was one of the main founders of Arabian literature, and one of the pioneers of the new Arabian literature in the 20th century.

解析 Interpretation

该句展现了纪伯伦关心的文学议题——爱与美、人道主义、世界和平等。他认为，祖国和世界不是对立的两个概念，而是统一的。他反对假借“爱国主义”之名的侵略行为，认为整个人类如同一家人，应该相亲相爱、和平共处。

This quote shows Gibran's most concerned literary issues: love and beauty, humanitarianism, world peace and so on. He thinks that one's motherland and the world are not two opposite concepts, but unified. He opposes aggression provoked in the name of "patriotism", and thinks the whole human race is like a family, who should love each other and live in peace.

25

القلوب سواقي.

译文 Translated Text

人心都是相通的。

People are linked to each other by heart.

作者及出处 Author and Source

杨言洪主编《阿拉伯语汉语成语谚语辞典》。

A Dictionary of Arabic and Chinese Idioms and Proverbs, Ed. Yang Yanhong.

解析 Interpretation

这句谚语原意为“人心如水渠”，指人们的心如同水渠一样，是联结在一起的，引申为“人心都是相通的”。

The original meaning of this proverb is “people’s hearts are like canals”, which means that people’s hearts are connected with each other like canals, and is extended in meaning as “people are linked to each other by heart”.

六 日语名句

26

山川異域、風月同天。

译文 Translated Text

我们虽在不同的地域，但是仰首望去，你我共处同一片青天，共享同一轮明月。

Although we live in different regions, when looking up, you and I share the same blue sky and the same bright moon.

作者及出处 Author and Source

长屋王（長屋王）的诗歌《绣袈裟衣缘》。

Prince Nagaya, the poem "Karma Knitted in the Cassocks" .

背景简介 Background Knowledge

长屋王（684—729），日本奈良时代（710—794）的皇族、著名政治家。

Prince Nagaya (684–729) was an imperial prince of Japan and famous politician of the Nara Period (710–794).

解析 Interpretation

这两句话表达的意思是：你我虽然身处不同的地方，但彼此拥有同样的体会和感受。

The meaning of these two lines is: Although you and I live in different places, we have the same experience and feeling.

27

世界全体が幸福にならないうちは、個人の幸福はありえない。

译文 Translated Text

没有全人类的幸福就没有个人的幸福。

Without the happiness of all mankind, there would be no happiness of individuals.

作者及出处 Author and Source

宫泽贤治（宮沢賢治）《【新】校本宫泽贤治全集　第十三卷（上）觉书·手帐 本文篇》。

Miyazawa Kenji, *The Collated Edition of the Complete Works of Miyazawa Kenji*, Vol. 13 (Part I).

背景简介 Background Knowledge

宫泽贤治（1896—1933），日本昭和时代（1926—1989）早期的童话作家、诗人、教育家、词作家、农业指导家。

Miyazawa Kenji (1896–1933) was a fairy tale writer, poet, educator, lyricist and agricultural director in the early Showa Period (1926–1989) of Japan.

解析 Interpretation

出于对他人以及人世间苦难的悲悯，宫泽贤治把别人的快乐当成自己的快乐，把别人的痛苦当成自己的痛苦。他认为，站在他人的角度看问题，并在他人需要的时候伸出援助之手，这是让整个世界都幸福的前提；没有全世界、全人类的幸福，也就谈不上个人的幸福。

Out of compassion for others and the suffering of people in the world, Miyazawa Kenji regards the happiness of others as his own happiness and the pain of others as his own pain. He believes that seeing things from the perspective of others and reaching out one's hands to help others when they are in need is the prerequisite of making the whole world happy. Without the happiness of the whole world, there would be no happiness of individuals.

七 朝鲜语名句

28

근본 원리는 사람과 멀리 떨어져 있지 않고 사람은 나라가 달라도 모두 똑같다 .

汉语原文及英文译文 Original Text in Chinese and Translated Text

道不远人，人无异国。

Great distance cannot separate us; we all live in a united world.

作者及出处 Author and Source

崔致远《真鉴禅师碑铭》。

Choe Chiwon, “Memorial Stele to Master Jingam” .

背景简介 Background Knowledge

崔致远（857—不详），新罗末期人，是朝鲜半岛历史上第一位留下了个人文集的大学者、诗人，被朝鲜和韩国的学术界尊奉为“汉文学的开山鼻祖”，有“东国儒宗”“东国文学之祖”之称。崔致远著述“道不远人，人无异国”这句话使用的是汉语，后译为朝鲜语并成为广为人知的名言。

Choe Chiwon (857–year of death unknown), living at the end of the Silla Period, was the first scholar and poet in Korean history who left a personal anthology. He was honored as “the founder of Chinese literature in Korea” by the Korean academic circles, and referred to as “the forefather of the Confucian School in Korea” and “the progenitor of Korean literature” . Choe Chiwon wrote the sentence “道不远人，人无异国” in Chinese, which was translated into Korean and became a well-known saying.

解析 Interpretation

这句话是说：国与国之间虽然存在多方面的差异，但人们的心灵却是彼此相通的，人们可以通过互相尊重和理解而成为一家人。

This quote means that although there are many differences between countries, people are linked to each other by heart, and they can become one family through mutual respect and understanding.

第二部分

和平相处

一 汉语名句

29

有朋自远方来，不亦乐乎？

译文 Translated Text

有志同道合的人从远方来，不也很快乐吗？

Is it not delightful to have friends coming from afar?

作者及出处 Author and Source

《论语·学而》。

The Analects (Book I, Xue Er).

背景简介 Background Knowledge

《论语》是孔子弟子及再传弟子为记录孔子及其弟子言行而编成的语录集，较为集中地体现了孔子及儒家学派的政治主张、伦理思想、道德观念及教育原则。孔子（公元前 551—公元前 479），中国古代思想家、政治家、教育家，儒家学派创始人。

The Analects is a collection of quotations compiled by Confucius' disciples and his disciples' disciples to record the words and deeds of Confucius and his disciples. It embodies the political views, ethical thoughts, moral concepts and educational principles of Confucius and the Confucian School. Confucius (551 B.C.–479 B.C.) was an ancient Chinese thinker, statesman, educator, and founder of the Confucian School in the Spring and Autumn Period.

解析 Interpretation

这句话表明了中国人对待远方来客的态度。世界各国的人来到中国，与中国合作交流，中国人是很喜悦、很欢迎的。中国人乐意敞开大门，和世界各国人民交朋友。只有这样，世界才能真正认识中国，中国才能更加了解世界。

This quote shows the welcoming attitude of the Chinese people in general towards friends coming from afar. The Chinese people are very happy and welcoming when people from all over the world come to China for cooperation and exchange. They are willing to open their doors and make friends with people from all corners of the earth. Only in this way can the world really understand China and China know the world better.

30

礼之用，和为贵。

译文 Translated Text

礼仪的使用，归根到底是为了以礼求和，通过礼仪秩序来使人与人之间的关系变得和谐。

Practicing the rules of propriety is for the preciousness of harmony.

作者及出处 Author and Source

《论语·学而》。

The Analects (Book I, Xue Er).

背景简介 Background Knowledge

《论语》是孔子弟子及再传弟子为记录孔子及其弟子言行而编成的语录集，较为集中地体现了孔子及儒家学派的政治主张、伦理思想、道德观念及教育原则。孔子（公元前 551—公元前 479），中国古代思想家、政治家、教育家，儒家学派创始人。

The Analects is a collection of quotations compiled by Confucius' disciples and his disciples' disciples to record the words and deeds of Confucius and his disciples. It embodies the political

views, ethical thoughts, moral concepts and educational principles of Confucius and the Confucian School. Confucius (551 B.C.–479 B.C.) was an ancient Chinese thinker, statesman, educator, and founder of the Confucian School in the Spring and Autumn Period.

解析 Interpretation

中国自古就是礼仪之邦，礼在中国社会中发挥着非常重要的作用。孔子说“礼以行之”，就是说君子要以礼作为行动的规范。事实上，礼仪规范只是外在形式，真正的目的是要达到和谐，“和为贵”才是礼的精神内核。天下一家、协和万邦是中华文明的理想愿景，爱好和平、追求和谐是中国人的悠久传统。直到今天，这种“和为贵”的思想仍然为人们深深认同和传承。2014年5月15日，习近平主席在中国国际友好大会暨中国人民对外友好协会成立60周年纪念活动上的讲话中指出：“在5000多年的文明发展中，中华民族一直追求和传承着和平、和睦、和谐的坚定理念。以和为贵，与人为善，己所不欲、勿施于人等理念在中国代代相传，深深植根于中国人的精神中，深深体现在中国人的行为上。”

China has been a country of propriety since ancient times. Propriety plays a very important role in Chinese society. Confucius said that “we should pursue righteousness according to propriety”, that is to say, a gentleman should take propriety as the norm of action. In fact, propriety is only an external form, and the real purpose is to achieve harmony. The spiritual core of “propriety” lies in “the preciousness of harmony” . It is a long-cherished prospect of Chinese civilization that “all people under heaven are of one family” and that “peace and harmony should prevail” . Loving peace and pursuing harmony is a time-honored tradition of the Chinese people. Up to now, the idea of “the preciousness of harmony” is still deeply recognized and inherited by people. On May 15, 2014, at China International Friendship Conference in Commemoration of the 60th Anniversary of the Chinese People's Association for Friendship with Foreign Countries, President Xi Jinping said, “In the past 5,000 years' development of civilization, the Chinese nation has been pursuing and inheriting the firm concept of peace, amity and harmony. The concepts of ‘the preciousness of harmony’ , ‘kindness to others’ , and ‘avoiding doing to others what you would not have them do to you’ have been passed down from generation to generation in China, deeply rooted in the spirit of the Chinese people and well reflected in their behaviors. ”

二
英语名句

31

Peace cannot be kept by force; it can only be achieved by understanding.

译文 Translated Text

和平不能靠武力来维持，只有通过理解才能获得。

作者及出处 Author and Source

阿尔伯特·爱因斯坦，选自爱丽丝·卡拉普里斯所著的《爱因斯坦新名言》。

Albert Einstein, from *The New Quotable Einstein* by Alice Calaprice.

背景简介 Background Knowledge

阿尔伯特·爱因斯坦（1879—1955），德裔美国物理学家，1921 年诺贝尔物理学奖获得者，被美国《时代周刊》评选为 20 世纪的“世纪伟人”。同时，爱因斯坦也是 20 世纪初欧洲和平运动的发起人之一。

Albert Einstein (1879–1955) was a German-American physicist, the winner of the 1921 Nobel Prize in Physics, and was named the “person of the 20th century” by *Time* magazine. He was also one of the founders of the peace movement in Europe at the beginning of the 20th century.

解析 Interpretation

选句出自爱因斯坦 1930 年 12 月 14 日为“新历史学会”所做的演讲。他谴责战争造成的社会动荡，向往一个不同国家之间互相理解、和平共处的世界。

This quote is from Einstein’s speech to the New History Society on December 14, 1930, in which he condemned war as a cause of social unrest and showed his yearning for a world in which different countries can understand each other and co-exist in peace.

32

I don't want to rule or conquer anyone. I should like to help everyone, if possible, Jew, gentile, black man, white. We all want to help one another. Human beings are like that. We want to live by each other's happiness – not by each other's misery. We don't want to hate and despise one another.

译文 Translated Text

我不想统治或征服任何人。如果可能的话，我想帮助所有人，不管是犹太人还是非犹太人，是黑人还是白人，我们都想互相帮助。人类就是这样，我们希望依靠彼此的幸福来生活，而不希望依靠彼此的痛苦来生活。我们不想互相憎恨和鄙视。

作者及出处 Author and Source

查理·卓别林，电影《大独裁者》中“理发师的演讲”。

Charlie Chaplin, “The Final Speech” from the movie *The Great Dictator*.

背景简介 Background Knowledge

查理·卓别林（1889—1977），英国喜剧演员、导演及反战人士。

Charlie Chaplin (1889–1977) was a British comedian, director and anti-war activist.

解析 Interpretation

《大独裁者》（1940）是由卓别林导演并主演的一部电影。影片以第二次世界大战为背景，塑造了一个残酷迫害犹太人、企图统治全世界的大独裁者形象，并对这个人物进行了辛辣的讽刺，对其所代表的法西斯主义、反犹太主义和纳粹进行了强烈的谴责。“理发师的演讲”出现于影片最后，演讲呼吁民主与正义，表达了人们内心对人人平等、各个种族和睦共处的渴望。

The Great Dictator (1940) is a movie directed and starred by Chaplin. Set in the Second World War, the film portrays a great dictator who persecuted Jews cruelly and attempted to reign on the earth. The film also makes a bitter satire on this character and strongly condemns the fascism, anti-Semitism and Nazism he represents. “The Final Speech” appears at the end of the film. The speech calls for democracy and justice, expressing people’s inner desire for equality and harmonious coexistence of all races.

33

Nonviolence is the greatest force at the disposal of mankind. It is mightier than the mightiest weapon of destruction devised by the ingenuity of man.

译文 Translated Text

非暴力是人类可以支配的最伟大的力量，它比人类用聪明才智设计出来的最强大的毁灭性武器还要强大。

作者及出处 Author and Source

莫汉达斯·卡拉姆昌德·甘地《四海之内皆兄弟：自传体反思录》。

Mohandas Karamchand Gandhi, *All Men Are Brothers: Autobiographical Reflections*.

背景简介 Background Knowledge

莫汉达斯·卡拉姆昌德·甘地（1869—1948），印度政治家、革命家、思想家，被称为“印度国父”。

Mohandas Karamchand Gandhi (1869–1948) was an Indian statesman, revolutionary and thinker, and is referred to as “Father of the Indian Nation” .

解析 Interpretation

甘地坚持追求“非暴力”的理念。他认为，爱是人的本性，人类的爱才是世界上最强大的存在。天下一家亲，人类施加于人类的暴行是不允许存在的。甘地这句话表达了和平共处的主题。

Gandhi was committed to the pursuit of the notion of non-violence. He believed that love was part of the human nature and human love was the most powerful force in the world. All people under heaven are of one family, and there is no place for human atrocities committed against humanity. The theme of peaceful coexistence is expressed in Gandhi's remark.

34

Imagine all the people
Living life in peace...
You may say I'm a dreamer,
But I'm not the only one.
I hope someday you'll join us,
And the world will live as one.

译文 Translated Text

想象所有的人
生活在和平之中……
也许你会说我是一个空想者，
但拥有这种想法的并非仅我一人。
我希望有一天你也能与我们为伍，
我们将实现世界大同。

作者及出处 Author and Source

约翰·列侬的歌曲《想象》。

John Lennon, the song "Imagine" .

背景简介 Background Knowledge

约翰·列侬（1940—1980），英国歌手和词曲作者，“披头士”乐队成员，和平主义者。

John Lennon (1940–1980) was a British singer, songwriter and member of the Beatles. He was also a peace activist.

解析 Interpretation

这几句词出自约翰·列侬创作的歌曲《想象》。歌曲呼吁人们去想象一个没有战火、没有宗教派别、没有民族界限的和谐世界，表达了作者对一个没有杀戮、没有歧视的和平世界的期盼。

The selected lyrics are taken from the song “Imagine” written and sung by John Lennon. The song calls on people to imagine a harmonious world without war, religious sects or ethnic boundaries, expressing the author’s expectations for a peaceful world without killing or discrimination.

三

法语名句

35

Il n'y a pas de loi qui puisse régir l'harmonie entre les êtres. Elle ne peut être réalisée que par un effort constant de chacun.

译文 Translated Text

没有任何法则可以支配人与人之间的和谐，只有所有人不懈努力才能实现和谐。

There is no law that can control the harmony between people. It can only be achieved by the unremitting efforts of all people.

作者及出处 Author and Source

艾瑞卡·琼，与苏菲·拉纳的会谈（1978 年 7—8 月）。

Erica Jong, talk with Sophie Lannes from July to August in 1978.

背景简介 Background Knowledge

艾瑞卡·琼，生于 1942 年，是美国 20 世纪 70 年代涌现出的典型的女性主义作家之一，其诗歌和小说都具有明显的女性主义色彩。

Erica Jong (born in 1942) is one of the representative feminist writers emerging in the 1970s in the United States, whose poems and novels have distinctive feminist features.

解析 Interpretation

这句名言旨在强调人类和平相处的重要性。

This quote aims to emphasize the importance of peaceful coexistence among people.

36

Pour qu'il y ait la paix sur la terre, il faudra que tous les êtres soient intérieurement en paix.

译文 Translated Text

只有众生内部和平，整个地球才能实现和平。

Only if there is peace among all living beings, can the whole earth achieve peace.

作者及出处 Author and Source

克劳德·什涅《最后通牒》。

Claude Chénier, *Ultimatum*.

背景简介 Background Knowledge

克劳德·什涅，加拿大作家。

Claude Chénier is a Canadian writer.

解析 Interpretation

为了实现世界和平，地球上的所有生灵都应和谐共处、拒绝战争。世界万物是和谐统一的命运共同体。

In order to achieve world peace, all living creatures on the earth should live in harmony, avert wars and become a community of shared future.

四
西班牙语名句

37

Desearía que se desarrollara en todos los pueblos un consciente sentido de paz y el sentimiento de solidaridad humana, que puedan abrir nuevas relaciones de respeto e igualdad para el próximo milenio, que deberá ser de fraternidad y no de conflictos cruentos.

译文 Translated Text

我期待各国人民能自觉拥有和平意识和团结精神，在新千年建立起互相尊重、彼此平等的新关系，大家亲如手足，不再有血腥冲突。

I look forward to the people from all countries self-consciously having a sense of peace and a spirit of unity, and establishing a new relationship of mutual respect and equality in the new millennium. We are close like brothers, and there will be no more bloody conflicts.

作者及出处 Author and Source

里戈韦塔·门楚·图姆。

Rigoberta Menchú Tum.

背景简介 Background Knowledge

里戈韦塔·门楚·图姆，生于1959年，危地马拉政治家。因长期致力于改善危地马拉土著人民的生活状况，她于1992年获得诺贝尔和平奖。

Rigoberta Menchú Tum (born in 1959) is a Guatemalan political and human rights activist, who won the Nobel Peace Prize in 1992 for her long-term efforts to improve the living conditions of the Guatemalan indigenous people.

解析 Interpretation

图姆的这句话是希望人类能达成这样的广泛共识：世界需要和平、需要友爱。和平的核心是安全和繁荣，这意味着人们不再处于动乱和恐慌之中，意味着社会进步发展能给大家创造日益美好的生活。世界和平需要各国人民彼此尊重、亲如一家，团结起来共同实现人类的美好愿望。

Tum's remark shows the hope that mankind can reach such a broad consensus, that is, the world needs peace, friendship and love. The core of peace is security and prosperity, which means that people will no longer be in turmoil and panic, and that social progress and development can create an increasingly better life for all. World peace requires people from all countries to respect each other, be close as one family, and unite to realize the good expectations of mankind.

五 阿拉伯语名句

38

الخصومة تورث العداوة، والوئام يورث الصداقة.

译文 Translated Text

两斗皆仇，两和皆友。

Fighting on both sides leads to enmity while harmony leads to friendship.

作者及出处 Author and Source

杨言洪主编《阿拉伯语汉语成语谚语辞典》。

A Dictionary of Arabic and Chinese Idioms and Proverbs, Ed. Yang Yanhong.

解析 Interpretation

这句谚语原意为“争斗生仇隙，和睦结友谊”，强调说明人与人之间、国与国之间的交往，应该做到彼此尊重、平等相待、互相理解、互相体谅。只有这样，才能化解矛盾，达到和平共处的目的。

The original meaning of the proverb is that “fighting results in feuds and harmony leads to friendship”. The proverb emphasizes that people and countries are supposed to respect each other, treat each other equally, understand each other and forgive each other. Only in this way can we resolve contradictions and achieve the goal of harmonious and peaceful coexistence.

第三部分

睦邻友好

一

汉语名句

39

水之积也不厚，则其负大舟也无力。

译文 Translated Text

如果水积得不厚不深，那么它就没有力量承载起大船。

If water is not piled up deep enough, it won't have the strength to bear up a big boat.

作者及出处 Author and Source

庄子《庄子·逍遥游》。

Chuang Tzu, *Enjoyment in Untroubled Ease*.

背景简介 Background Knowledge

庄子（约公元前 369—公元前 286），战国时期的思想家、哲学家、文学家，道家学派代表人物，与老子并称“老庄”。

Chuang Tzu (c. 369 B.C.–286 B.C.) was a pivotal figure of Taoism, thinker, philosopher and writer during the Warring States Period. Lao Tzu and Chuang Tzu together are called “Lao-Chuang”.

解析 Interpretation

这句话是庄子的一个绝妙比喻，用水之“积厚”来形象地说明只有夯实深厚的根基，才能成就伟大的事业。2013 年 6 月 5 日，习近平主席在墨西哥参议院发表演讲时曾引用这句名言，揭示普通民众的直接交往是加深国与国友谊最有效的方式，普通民众的友好感情是推动国与国关系持久发展的不竭动力。

This is a wonderful metaphor of Chuang Tzu, which makes use of the “accumulated depth” of water to vividly show that only by consolidating the solid foundation, can a great cause be achieved. On June 5, 2013, President Xi Jinping quoted this famous saying in the speech delivered at the Mexican Senate, revealing that the direct contact between common people is the most effective way to deepen the friendship between different countries, and the friendly feelings of the common people are the inexhaustible driving force to promote the lasting development of the relationship between different countries.

40

合抱之木，生于毫末；九层之台，起于累土。

译文 Translated Text

粗壮得需要两臂围拢才能抱住的大树，是由细如毫发的幼苗生长起来的；层层叠叠的高台，是由泥土一点点堆筑而成的。

A big tree grows from a small seedling; and a nine-storeyed tower is built out of soil.

作者及出处 Author and Source

老子《老子·第六十四章》。

Lao Tzu, *Lao Tzu* (Chapter 64).

背景简介 Background Knowledge

老子（生卒年不详），春秋时期的思想家、哲学家，道家学派的创始人和主要代表人物，曾被列为世界文化名人，世界百位历史名人之一。

Lao Tzu (years of birth and death unknown) was a thinker and philosopher in the Spring and Autumn Period. He was also the founder and main representative of the Taoist School, and has been listed as one of the world cultural celebrities and one of the world's 100 historical celebrities.

解析 Interpretation

这句话揭示了一个道理：事物的发展都有一个逐渐变化的过程，由小到大，积少成多。国与国之间的交往也不例外。2013 年 10 月 3 日，习近平主席在印度尼西亚国会发表的演讲中曾引用这句话，表明中国与东盟国家之间的良好交往，必须建立在普通民众心心相印的基础之上，离不开中国与东盟各国青年、智库、议会、非政府组织、社会团体等的友好交流带来的相互了解和友谊，离不开科教文卫事业的交流互助。只有交往多了，感情深了，心与心才能贴得更近。

This quote suggests that there is a process of gradual change in the development of things, from small to large, every little making a mickle, and the communication between countries is no exception. On October 3, 2013, President Xi Jinping quoted this saying in the speech delivered at the Indonesian Parliament, pointing out that good exchanges between China and the ASEAN countries must be built on the basis of mutual affinity of common people, and cannot do without the mutual understanding and friendship between China and the ASEAN countries brought by the friendly exchanges between youth, think tanks, parliaments, non-governmental organizations and social organizations, or without the exchange and mutual assistance of the causes of education, science, culture and health. Only by more contacts and deeper feelings, can the hearts be closer.

41

亲望亲好，邻望邻好。

译文 Translated Text

乡亲邻里之间，彼此都希望对方幸福美满。

Neighbors wish each other well, just as loved ones do to each other.

作者及出处 Author and Source

郝长留编著《常用俗语词典》。

A Dictionary of Common Sayings, Ed. Hao Changliu.

背景简介 Background Knowledge

中国人重视邻里关系，因而产生了很多与之相关的俗语，如“亲帮亲，邻帮邻”“亲望亲好，邻望邻好”“亲向亲，邻向邻”等，这些俗语都表达同一个意思，那就是“邻里互助，和谐相处”。

Chinese people attach great importance to neighborhood relations, resulting in many related common sayings, such as “neighbors help each other like loved ones” , “neighbors wish each other well, just as loved ones do to each other” , “neighbors treat each other well like loved ones” and so on, all of which express the same meaning, that is, neighbors help each other and live in harmony.

解析 Interpretation

乡亲邻里，一则都是故乡人，二则比邻而居，所以关系密切，彼此都会希望对方幸福美满。邻国之间亦然。2013 年 4 月 7 日，习近平主席在博鳌亚洲论坛 2013 年年会上的主旨演讲中曾引用此语，表明中国将坚持与邻为善、以邻为伴，巩固睦邻友好，深化互利合作，努力使自身发展更好惠及周边国家。他指出："亲仁善邻，是中国自古以来的传统。"近年来，中国与周边国家携手互助，患难与共，让命运共同体的意识不断落地生根。

Neighbors live next to each other and thus share a close relationship. They wish each other well, and the same is true for our relationship with neighboring countries. On April 7, 2013, President Xi Jinping quoted this saying in the keynote speech delivered at the Boao Forum for Asia annual conference, making it clear that China will adhere to the policy of building a good-neighborly relationship and partnership with its neighbors, deepening mutually beneficial cooperation, and striving to make its own development be of benefit to the neighboring countries. He pointed out that "it has been a tradition of China since ancient times to be kind to benevolent people and its neighbors." In recent years, China and its neighboring countries have worked hand in hand to help each other and share weal and woe, so that the consciousness of a community of shared future has gradually become deep-rooted.

42

德不孤，必有邻。

译文 Translated Text

有道德的人是不会孤单的，一定会有志同道合的人来与他为伴、为邻。

Moral and virtuous people do not feel lonely, because like-minded people will accompany them.

作者及出处 Author and Source

《论语·里仁》。

The Analects (Book IV, Li Ren).

背景简介 Background Knowledge

《论语》是孔子弟子及再传弟子为记录孔子及其弟子言行而编成的语录集，较为集中地体现了孔子及儒家学派的政治主张、伦理思想、道德观念及教育原则。孔子（公元前551—公元前479），中国古代思想家、政治家、教育家，儒家学派创始人。

The Analects is a collection of quotations compiled by Confucius' disciples and his disciples' disciples to record the words and deeds of Confucius and his disciples. It embodies the political

views, ethical thoughts, moral concepts and educational principles of Confucius and the Confucian School. Confucius (551 B.C.–479 B.C.) was an ancient Chinese thinker, statesman, educator, and founder of the Confucian School in the Spring and Autumn Period.

解析 Interpretation

“德”指品行、德行，是人们共同遵循的行为准则和道义规范。这句话是说，只要一个人遵守社会的行为准则和道德规范，具有良好的道德品质，就一定会有人来与他结为邻居、伙伴。国家也是一样。一个国家只要有德行，遵守国际准则和人类道义，就不会孤立，必然会有好邻居、好伙伴与之和睦相处，共同发展。

“Virtue” refers to moral conduct and integrity, which is the code of conduct and moral norm followed by people in general. This quote means that as long as a person abides by the social code of conduct and moral standards and has high moral quality, there will be someone to be his neighbor or partner. The same is true for a country. As long as a country has “virtue” and abides by international norms and human morality, it will not be isolated. It will certainly have good neighbors and partners with whom to live in harmony and develop together.

43

亲仁善邻，国之宝也。

译文 Translated Text

亲近仁义，和邻国友好相处，这是国家的宝贵财富。

It is a valuable asset of the country to be kind to benevolent people and its neighbors.

作者及出处 Author and Source

左丘明《左传·隐公六年》。

Zuo Qiuming, *Commentary on Spring and Autumn Annals by Zuo Qiuming* (The Sixth Year of Lord Yin).

背景简介 Background Knowledge

左丘明（约公元前 502—约公元前 422），春秋末期史学家、文学家、思想家。

Zuo Qiuming (c. 502 B.C.–422 B.C.) was a historian, writer and thinker in the late Spring and Autumn Period.

解析 Interpretation

中国在历史上形成了深厚的农耕文化传统，中国人一般都安土重迁，因此“邻里”作为一种以地缘因素为基础而形成的人际关系，对中国人来说具有十分重要的意义。中国人重信义、讲情义，重视与邻邦之间的和睦相处、守望相助，也重视与不同文明之间的交流互鉴、协调合作。这不仅是中国人的处世之道，也是中华民族追求的理想目标。

China has formed a profound cultural tradition of farming in history, and Chinese people are generally content with their native places, not willing to move house easily. Therefore, as a kind of interpersonal relationship formed on the basis of regional factors, “neighborhood” is of great significance to the Chinese people. The Chinese people attach great importance to faithfulness and friendship, harmonious coexistence and mutual help between neighbors and neighboring countries, as well as exchanges, mutual learning, coordination and cooperation with different civilizations. This is not only the philosophy of life of the Chinese people, but also the ideal goal pursued by the Chinese nation.

44

海内存知己，天涯若比邻。

译文 Translated Text

知心朋友即使远在天涯海角，只要朋友情深，也会感觉像近邻一样。

Even if close friends stay very far away from each other, they feel like close neighbors as long as they are affectionate in relationship.

作者及出处 Author and Source

王勃的诗歌《送杜少府之任蜀州》。

Wang Bo, the poem "Farewell to Prefect Du" .

背景简介 Background Knowledge

王勃（约 650—676），唐代诗人，"初唐四杰"之一。

Wang Bo (c. 650–676) was a poet in the Tang Dynasty, one of the "Four Literary Eminences in the Early Tang Dynasty" .

解析 Interpretation

这两句诗表达的意思是：友谊不受时间的限制和空间的阻

隔，真正的知己朋友即使远在天涯海角，也会如同近邻一样心意相通。不同国家的人们可能相隔万里之遥，但人们之间的情谊不会因距离而隔绝。人类是一个命运共同体，人类共同的情感可以跨越时空的限制，不同国家的人们能够相知相守，团结合作，共同发展。

These two lines express the idea that friendship is not restricted by time, nor obstructed by space. True confidants or bosom friends, even if they live very far away from each other, will feel interlinked mentally just like close neighbors. People in different countries may be thousands of miles away, but the friendship between them will never be separated by distance. Human beings are a community of shared future and their common emotions can transcend the limitation of time and space, so that people in different countries can know each other, be united, cooperate and develop together.

二
英语名句

45

The highest education is that which does not merely give us information, but makes our life in harmony with all existence.

译文 Translated Text

最高程度的教育不仅仅是向我们传授知识，还要教会我们与他人及万物和谐共生。

作者及出处 Author and Source

拉宾德拉纳特 · 泰戈尔，转引自帕特里克 · 科尔姆 · 霍根和拉丽塔 · 潘迪特所著的《拉宾德拉纳特 · 泰戈尔：普遍性和传统》。

Rabindranath Tagore, from *Rabindranath Tagore: Universality and Tradition* by Patrick Colm Hogan and Lalita Pandit.

背景简介 Background Knowledge

拉宾德拉纳特·泰戈尔（1861—1941），印度诗人、文学家、社会活动家、哲学家。他是第一位获得诺贝尔文学奖的亚洲人。

Rabindranath Tagore (1861–1941) was an Indian poet, writer, social activist, and philosopher. He was the first Asian writer to win the Nobel Prize in Literature.

解析 Interpretation

泰戈尔认为，教育不仅要植根于人们周围的环境，而且应该与更广阔的世界相关联。这句话很好地体现了人与人、人与自然和谐共处的主题。

Tagore believes that education should not only be deeply rooted in one's immediate surroundings, but also be connected to the wider world. This quote well embodies the theme of harmonious coexistence between man and man, as well as man and nature.

46

There, in one single word, is the resolve which the forces of freedom and progress, of tolerance and good will, should take.

译文 Translated Text

一言以蔽之，我们应该下定决心去争取获得自由和进步、宽容和善意的力量。

作者及出处 Author and Source

温斯顿·丘吉尔《在战争中》。

Winston Churchill, *Into Battle*.

背景简介 Background Knowledge

温斯顿·丘吉尔（1874—1965），英国保守党领袖，曾于1940年至1945年和1951年至1955年两度担任英国首相。

Winston Churchill (1874–1965) was the leader of the British Conservative Party, who served as British Prime Minister from 1940 to 1945 and from 1951 to 1955.

解析 Interpretation

这段话源自丘吉尔于 1938 年 10 月 16 日对美国发表的广播演说《捍卫自由与和平》。演说展现了丘吉尔对人民之间和国家之间自由、平等、和平共处的期望。

This quote is taken from Churchill's broadcast speech "The Defence of Freedom and Peace", which was delivered to the United States from London on October 16, 1938. The speech showed Churchill's expectation of freedom, equality and peaceful coexistence among people and all countries.

三 法语名句

47

Nous n’avons pas besoin de fraternités communautaires, mais d’une fraternité universelle.

译文 Translated Text

我们需要的不是群体小爱，而是世间大爱。

What we need is not fraternity within a small community, but universal fraternity among people all over the world.

作者及出处 Author and Source

阿布登诺·比达尔，2015 年 1 月 23 日《费加罗报》。

Abdennour Bidar, in *Figaro*, January 23, 2015.

背景简介 Background Knowledge

阿布登诺 · 比达尔，生于 1971 年，法国哲学家、散文家，法国高级官员。

Abdennour Bidal (born in 1971) is a French philosopher, essayist, and senior official.

解析 Interpretation

“世间大爱”指的是不同民族、不同国家的人应该博爱，应该和睦相处，这正是“天下一家”的思想。

“Universal fraternity among people all over the world” refers to the idea that people from different nations and countries should have universal love and live in harmony, which is similar to the Chinese concept that “all people under heaven are of one family” .

四 俄语名句

48

Дружно – не грузно, а один и у каши загинет.

译文 Translated Text

众人干活儿不觉累，一人吃饭也不香。

People don't feel tired when they work together, and one doesn't enjoy the meal when he or she eats alone.

作者及出处 Author and Source

弗·伊·达里《俄罗斯民间谚语》。

Vladimir Ivanovich Dal, *Proverbs of the Russian People*.

背景简介 Background Knowledge

弗·伊·达里（1801—1872），俄国学者、作家、语言学家、医生，俄罗斯历史上最重要的辞书之一《现代大俄罗斯语详解辞典》的编纂者，《俄罗斯民间谚语》的作者。

Vladimir Ivanovich Dal (1801–1872) was a Russian scholar, writer, linguist and doctor. He was the compiler of the *Explanatory*

Dictionary of the Living Great Russian Language, one of the most important dictionaries in Russian history, and the author of *Proverbs of the Russian People*.

解析 Interpretation

此条谚语通过对集体和个人关系的比较，给人以启示。在和谐的集体中，人们和睦相处、包容互尊，更能激发出共同前进的力量，再复杂的工作都能够胜任，再大的困难都可以克服。

This proverb gives people enlightenment by comparing the relationships between the collective and the individuals. In a harmonious collective relationship, people can live in harmony, tolerate and respect each other, which can stimulate the power for common progress. No matter how complicated the work is, they can do it; no matter how great the difficulties are, they can overcome them.

五 西班牙语名句

49

La verdadera hermandad no requiere lazos de sangre.

译文 Translated Text

真正的兄弟不一定血脉相连。

True brothers are not necessarily connected by blood.

作者及出处 Author and Source

何塞·纳洛斯基，选自吉耶莫·姆拉伊编著的《名言警语集》(*Pintas: Frases de expresion urbana*)。

José Narosky, from *A Collection of Famous Sayings and Aphorisms* by Guillermo Murray.

背景简介 Background Knowledge

何塞·纳洛斯基，生于 1930 年，阿根廷作家。

José Narosky (born in 1930) is an Argentine writer.

解析 Interpretation

这句话是说，真正的兄弟并不一定需要血缘关系。言下之意，在世界范围里大家都可以成为好朋友、好兄弟、好姐妹，都可以和谐相处、共同发展。

What Narosky means is that true brothers do not necessarily need to be related by blood. The implication is that all people in the world can become good friends, good brothers and sisters, live in harmony and develop together.

50

Más vale amigos en la plaza, que dineros en el arca.

译文 Translated Text

广场上的朋友胜过箱子里的金钱。

Friends in the square are better than money in the box.

作者及出处 Author and Source

佚名，选自西班牙塞万提斯学院官方网站整理的谚语集锦。

Anonymous, from the collection of proverbs sorted out by the official website of Cervantes Institute.

解析 Interpretation

这句话背后的含义是：人类生活在同一个地球，为了共同建设这个美丽的家园，国家间、民族间应通过对话交流相互了解，像朋友一样真诚相待、共同进步。在此过程中建立起的深厚友谊和宝贵信任是真正的财富，是人类和平、繁荣发展的有力保障。

The implied meaning of this quote is that human beings live on the same earth, and in order to build this beautiful home together, all countries and nations should understand each other through dialogues and exchanges, treat each other sincerely like friends and keep forging ahead together. The deep friendship and precious trust established in this process are real treasure and a firm guarantee for the peaceful and prosperous development of humankind.

六 阿拉伯语名句

51

خذ لك من كل بلد صاحب ولا تاخذ من كل اقليم عدو.

译文 Translated Text

处处有宾朋，天下无敌人。

There are friends everywhere, and there are not enemies anywhere.

作者及出处 Author and Source

杨言洪主编《阿拉伯语汉语成语谚语辞典》。

A Dictionary of Arabic and Chinese Idioms and Proverbs, Ed. Yang Yanhong.

解析 Interpretation

该句原意为“宁可在每乡找一个朋友，不可在每地树一个敌人”，指每当去到一个地方时，都应与人为善、结交朋友，而不能与人结怨、树立仇敌。该句又可引申为“朋友千个少，敌人一个多”，意在强调与他人沟通交往时，应该以积极友好的态度去多结交朋友。

The original meaning of this proverb is that "it's better to find a friend in every town than to make an enemy in every place", which means that whenever you go to a new place, you should be kind to the local people and make friends with them, instead of incurring grudges and making enemies. It is extended in meaning to the saying "a thousand friends are not enough; one enemy is too many", which intends to emphasize that when communicating with others, we should make more friends with a friendly and positive attitude.

52

أطلب الخير لجارك تلقاه في دارك، واطلب الشر لجارك تلقاه في دارك.

译文 Translated Text

邻家有喜你沾光，邻家有难你倒霉。

When there is a happy event happening to your neighbor, you also enjoy the jubilant atmosphere; when your neighbor is in trouble, you are also affected.

作者及出处 Author and Source

杨言洪主编《阿拉伯语汉语成语谚语辞典》。

A Dictionary of Arabic and Chinese Idioms and Proverbs, Ed. Yang Yanhong.

解析 Interpretation

该句原意为“为邻居求好事，你在自家也会遇到好事；为邻居求坏事，你在自家也会遇到坏事”，指应该善待邻居，与邻居友好相处。该句又可引申为“盼邻居走运，自家也会走运；盼邻居遭殃，自家也会遭殃”，意在强调无论是小家之间还是国家之间，邻居、邻国都是和自身命运联系较为紧密的一部分，应该与邻居、邻国和谐友好地相处，相互帮助，相互扶持，谋求共同进步。

The original meaning of this proverb is that "if you pray for good things for your neighbors, good things will also happen to you; if you stir up trouble to your neighbors, you will also encounter bad things in your own house", which means that you should be kind to your neighbors and get along well with them. It is extended in meaning to the saying "if you wish your neighbors good luck, your own family will also be lucky; if you wish your neighbors bad luck, your own family will also be unlucky", which intends to emphasize that no matter it is between families or countries, neighbors are a part that is closely related to our own fate, so we should get along with our neighbors in a harmonious and friendly way, help and support each other, and pursue common progress.

第四部分

文明互鉴

一

汉语名句

53

五色交辉，相得益彰；八音合奏，终和且平。

译文 Translated Text

多种颜色交相辉映，各自的优点、特色便更加鲜明突出；各种声音一起合奏，在彼此交响中达到和谐与平衡。

Five colors, when shining upon each other, will add beauty to each other; eight musical instruments, when played together, will make a harmonious melody.

作者及出处 Author and Source

冯友兰《国立西南联合大学纪念碑碑文》。

Feng Youlan, “Inscription on the Monument of National Southwest Associated University” .

背景简介 Background Knowledge

冯友兰（1895—1990），中国著名哲学家。

Feng Youlan (1895–1990) was a famous Chinese philosopher.

解析 Interpretation

中国文化从源头上就具有多源共生、和而不同、兼容并包的特点。同理，人类文明也是丰富多彩的，各种文化之间应是兼容并蓄、求同存异、包容互鉴、和谐相处的。2014年6月5日，习近平主席在中阿合作论坛第六届部长级会议开幕式上的讲话中说："人类文明没有高低优劣之分，因为平等交流而变得丰富多彩，正所谓'五色交辉，相得益彰；八音合奏，终和且平'。"

From its source, the Chinese culture has the characteristics of multi-sourced coexistence, harmony without uniformity, and all-inclusiveness. Likewise, human civilization is also rich and colorful, and different cultures should be inclusive, seek common ground, respect differences, tolerate and learn from each other, and live in harmony. On June 5, 2014, in the speech delivered at the opening ceremony of the sixth ministerial meeting of the China-Arab States Cooperation Forum, President Xi Jinping said that "no one civilization can claim to be superior to others, and human civilization has become rich and colorful owing to the interaction on equal terms, so to speak, 'Five colors, when shining upon each other, will add beauty to each other; eight musical instruments, when played together, will make a harmonious melody.' "

54

物之不齐，物之情也。

译文 Translated Text

天下万物没有完全相同的，它们都有自己的独特个性，这是客观存在的。

Things are born to be different.

作者及出处 Author and Source

孟子《孟子·滕文公上》。

Mencius, *Mencius* (Duke Wen of Teng, Part I).

背景简介 Background Knowledge

孟子（约公元前372—公元前289），战国时期的哲学家、思想家、政治家、教育家，是孔子之后儒家学派的代表人物，与孔子并称“孔孟”。

Mencius (c. 372 B.C.–289 B.C.) was a philosopher, thinker, statesman and educator in the Warring States Period. He was the representative of the Confucian School after Confucius, and is referred to as “Confucius and Mencius” together with Confucius.

解析 Interpretation

孟子这句话强调了事物的差异性。物质世界如此，精神世界亦然。差异性是普遍存在的，不能以简单同一的标准来衡量事物的价值。2015 年 3 月 28 日，习近平主席在博鳌亚洲论坛 2015 年年会上的主旨演讲中曾引用这句话，并指出："不同文明没有优劣之分，只有特色之别。要促进不同文明不同发展模式交流对话，在竞争比较中取长补短，在交流互鉴中共同发展，让文明交流互鉴成为增进各国人民友谊的桥梁、推动人类社会进步的动力、维护世界和平的纽带。"

The quote from Mencius emphasizes the difference between things. This is true of the material world, as well as the spiritual world. Differences are ubiquitous and we cannot measure the value of different things by the same standard. On March 28, 2015, in the keynote speech delivered at the Boao Forum for Asia annual conference, President Xi Jinping quoted this saying to point out that "civilizations are only unique, and no one is superior to the other. There need to be more exchanges and dialogues between different civilizations and development models, so that we can learn from others' strong points to make up for our deficiencies through competition and comparison, and develop together by way of exchange and mutual learning. Let inter-civilization exchanges become the bridge of friendship for people from all countries, the driving force to promote the progress of human society, and the tie to safeguard the peace of the world."

55

和羹之美，在于合异。

译文 Translated Text

制作美味的羹汤，在于调和各种不同的滋味。

Delicious soup is made by combining different ingredients.

作者及出处 Author and Source

陈寿《三国志·夏侯玄传》。

Chen Shou, *Records of the Three Kingdoms* (Story of Xiahou Xuan).

背景简介 Background Knowledge

陈寿（233—297），西晋史学家。

Chen Shou (233–297) was a historian in the Western Jin Dynasty.

解析 Interpretation

一方水土养育一方人。中国幅员辽阔、历史悠久，不同地区形成了迥然有别的饮食特色，它们共同构成了中华民族博大精深的饮食文化。中国古人认为"酸、苦、辛、咸、甘"五味的调和因四时变化而有所不同，食物之美味正在于不同味道之间的调和。2017 年 1 月 18 日，习近平主席在联合国日内瓦总部发表的主旨演讲中曾引用这句话，以此强调坚持不同文明交流互鉴和建设一个开放包容世界的重要性。他指出："人类文明多样性是世界的基本特征，也是人类进步的源泉。世界上有 200 多个国家和地区、2500 多个民族、多种宗教。不同历史和国情，不同民族和习俗，孕育了不同文明，使世界更加丰富多彩。文明没有高下、优劣之分，只有特色、地域之别。文明差异不应该成为世界冲突的根源，而应该成为人类文明进步的动力。"

Each region has its own resources to support its own inhabitants. China has a vast territory and a long history and thus different regions have formed different food characteristics, which together constitute the extensive and profound food culture of the Chinese nation. The ancient people in China believed that the blending of the five flavors of "sourness, bitterness, spiciness, saltiness and sweetness" varied due to the change of seasons, and the deliciousness of food just depended on the blending of different flavors. In his keynote speech delivered at the headquarters of the United Nations in Geneva on January 18, 2017, President Xi Jinping quoted this saying as a metaphor to emphasize the importance of adhering to the exchanges and mutual learning between different civilizations and building an open and inclusive world. He pointed out that "the diversity of human civilization is the basic feature of the world and the source of human progress as well. There are over 200 countries and regions, over 2,500 ethnic groups, and various kinds of religions in the world. Different histories, national conditions, ethnicities and customs have bred different civilizations and made the world more colorful. Civilizations are only unique, and no one is superior to the other. Differences in civilization should not be the root cause of world conflicts, but the driving force of the progress of human civilization."

56

君子和而不同。

译文 Translated Text

君子在人际交往中能够与他人保持一种和谐友善的关系，但在对具体问题的看法上却不必苟同于对方。

In terms of interpersonal relationship, what a gentleman seeks is harmony instead of uniformity.

作者及出处 Author and Source

《论语·子路》。

The Analects (Book XIII, Zi Lu).

背景简介 Background Knowledge

《论语》是孔子弟子及再传弟子为记录孔子及其弟子言行而编成的语录集，较为集中地体现了孔子及儒家学派的政治主张、伦理思想、道德观念及教育原则。孔子（公元前551—公元前479），中国古代思想家、政治家、教育家，儒家学派创始人。

The Analects is a collection of quotations compiled by Confucius' disciples and his disciples' disciples to record the words and deeds of Confucius and his disciples. It embodies the political

views, ethical thoughts, moral concepts and educational principles of Confucius and the Confucian School. Confucius (551 B.C.–479 B.C.) was an ancient Chinese thinker, statesman, educator, and founder of the Confucian School in the Spring and Autumn Period.

解析 Interpretation

“和而不同”，简单地说就是和睦友善而不苟同。从孔子开始，“和而不同”就成为君子为人处世重要的道德规范和行为准则，后来更成为中国传统思想文化中最富生命力的文化核心原则。世界文明丰富多彩、各有特色，推进人类不同文明交流交融、互学互鉴，不同文明真正实现“和而不同”，才能让世界变得更加美丽，让各国民众的生活更加美好。

“Harmony instead of uniformity” simply means the friendly and harmonious relationship without hasty agreement before giving serious thought. Since the time of Confucius, this principle has become an important moral standard and code of conduct for a gentleman in society, and has later become the most vital core principle in traditional Chinese culture. The world civilizations are rich and colorful, and each has its own characteristics. Only by promoting the exchange, integration and mutual learning between different human civilizations and truly realizing “harmony instead of uniformity” among different civilizations, can the world become more beautiful and the people of all countries live a better life.

二
英语名句

57

If you have an apple and I have an apple and we exchange these apples then you and I will still each have one apple. But if you have an idea and I have an idea and we exchange these ideas, then each of us will have two ideas.

译文 Translated Text

如果你有一个苹果，我有一个苹果，我们互相交换，那么你和我仍然只会有一个苹果；但如果你有一个想法，我有一个想法，我们交换彼此的想法，那么我们每个人都会有两个想法。

作者及出处 Author and Source

乔治·萧伯纳，转引自迈克尔·尼尔所著的《你可以拥有你想要的东西：内在和外在成功的有效策略》。

George Bernard Shaw, from *You Can Have What You Want: Proven Strategies for Inner and Outer Success* by Michael Neill.

背景简介 Background Knowledge

乔治·萧伯纳（1856—1950），爱尔兰剧作家、小说家，1925 年诺贝尔文学奖获得者。

George Bernard Shaw (1856–1950) was an Irish playwright and novelist who won the Nobel Prize in Literature in 1925.

解析 Interpretation

萧伯纳意在强调要善于分享和交换彼此的观点，加强精神和思想上的交流，相互学习，取长补短。天下本为一家，我们应协力前进。这句话很好地体现了文明互鉴的主题。

The purpose of Bernard Shaw's remark is to promote sharing and exchanging ideas, to strengthen spiritual and ideological communication, to learn from each other, and to adopt others' strong points to make up for our deficiencies. All people under heaven are of one family, and we should advance together. This quote perfectly embodies the theme of mutual learning among different civilizations.

三
俄语名句

58

Чем более мы будем национальны, тем более мы будем европейцами.

译文 Translated Text

越是民族的，就越是世界的。

The more national, the more international.

作者及出处 Author and Source

费 · 米 · 陀思妥耶夫斯基，选自安德烈 · 拉夫鲁欣所著的《俄罗斯真理 · 格言》。

F. M. Dostoevsky, from *Russian Truths – Maxims* by Andrey Lavrushkin.

背景简介 Background Knowledge

费 · 米 · 陀思妥耶夫斯基（1821—1881），俄国作家、思想家、哲学家、评论家。

F. M. Dostoevsky (1821–1881) was a Russian writer, thinker, philosopher and critic.

解析 Interpretation

人类历史是由各民族共同书写的，璀璨文明是由各民族共同创造的，民族文化差异是人类命运共同体的基石。只有尊重各民族文化存在和发展的权利，尊重民族文化多样性，促进各民族文化并存互鉴，世界才能走向持久和平和普遍安全，人类才能实现全面发展和共同繁荣。

The history of mankind is written by and the resplendent culture is created by all nations. The differences between national cultures are the cornerstone of the community of shared future for mankind. Only by respecting the right of existence and development of all national cultures as well as the diversity of national cultures and promoting the coexistence and mutual learning of all cultures, can the world move towards lasting peace and universal security, and can human beings achieve the goal of all-round development and shared prosperity.

第五部分

包容互尊

一 汉语名句

59

海纳百川，有容乃大。

译文 Translated Text

大海之所以浩瀚无边，是因为容纳了一切河流的水。

The ocean is vast because it admits all rivers.

作者及出处 Author and Source

林则徐书两广总督府对联。

From the antithetical couplet written by Lin Zexu for the Governor's Office of Guangdong and Guangxi.

背景简介 Background Knowledge

林则徐（1785—1850），清代政治家、诗人。他对西方的文化、科技持开放态度，主张学其优而用之，主持编译《四洲志》，对晚清的洋务运动乃至日本的明治维新都具有启发作用。

Lin Zexu (1785–1850) was a statesman and poet in the Qing Dynasty. He held an open attitude to Western culture, science and technology. He advocated learning from their advantages and making use of them, and he was in charge of the translating and editing of Hugh Murray's *An Encyclopaedia of Geography*, which was enlightening to both the Self-Strengthening Movement in the late Qing Dynasty and the Meiji Restoration in Japan.

解析 Interpretation

这句话出自晚清名臣林则徐的一副自勉联——“海纳百川，有容乃大；壁立千仞，无欲则刚”，寓意是一个人要拥有像容纳无数江河之水的大海一样的宽阔胸襟。习近平主席 2013 年 10 月 3 日在印度尼西亚国会发表的演讲和 2017 年 1 月 18 日在联合国日内瓦总部发表的主旨演讲中都引用了这句话，表达出对世界各国都能包容共进、构建人类命运共同体的期待和信念。世界各国的命运是相互联系的，只有包容共进、和平发展、休戚与共，才能拥有美好的未来。

This quote is taken from a self-encouraging couplet by Lin Zexu, a famous minister in the late Qing Dynasty, which goes "The ocean is vast because it admits all rivers; the cliff stands upright steeply because it has no excessive desire" , implying that one should have a broad mind as the sea can contain countless rivers. In both the speech given to the Indonesian Parliament on October

3, 2013 and the keynote speech delivered at the headquarters of the United Nations in Geneva on January 18, 2017, President Xi Jinping quoted this line, showing the expectation and belief that all the countries in the world should be tolerant and make progress together, and build a community of shared future for mankind. The destinies of all countries in the world are interrelated and integrated. Only through inclusiveness, mutual progress, peaceful development, and sharing weal and woe, can we have a bright future.

60

万物并育而不相害，道并行而不相悖。

译文 Translated Text

天下万物竞相生长，但是彼此之间并不妨害；各种法则规律能同时运行而不相互矛盾。

All living things are nourished without injuring one another, and all roads run parallel without interfering with one another.

作者及出处 Author and Source

《礼记·中庸》。

The Book of Rites (Chapter XXXI, The Doctrine of the Mean).

背景简介 Background Knowledge

《礼记》是中国古代重要的典章制度选集，相传为西汉学者、礼学家戴圣编纂，主要记载先秦的礼制，体现了先秦儒家的哲学思想、教育思想、政治思想、美学思想，是研究先秦社会和儒家思想的重要资料。

The Book of Rites is an important anthology of ancient Chinese laws and regulations, purportedly compiled by the Western Han scholar and expert of Confucian ritual Dai Sheng. It mainly records the rites of the pre-Qin period, embodies the philosophy, education, politics and aesthetics of the pre-Qin Confucianism, and is an important material for the study of the pre-Qin society and Confucianism.

解析 Interpretation

这句话体现了中国古人对宇宙与自然法则的朴素认知，蕴含了中华文明包容并蓄、和而不同的价值追求。习近平主席2014年6月28日在和平共处五项原则发表60周年纪念大会上的讲话和2018年5月4日在纪念马克思诞辰200周年大会上的讲话中，两次引用这一名言，在新的时代背景下赋予其新的含义。他指出:“当今世界有70亿人口，200多个国家和地区，2500多个民族，5000多种语言。不同民族、不同文明多姿多彩、各有千秋，没有优劣之分，只有特色之别。”“我们要尊重文明多样性，推动不同文明交流对话、和平共处、和谐共生，不能唯我独尊、贬低其他文明和民族。”他还指出:“我们要站在世界历史的高度审视当今世界发展趋势和面临的重大问题，坚持和平发展道路，坚持独立自主的和平外交政策，坚持互利共赢的开放战略，不断拓展同世界各国的合作，积极参与全球治理，在更多领域、更高层面上实现合作共赢、共同发展，不依附别人、更不掠夺别人，同各国人民一道努力构建人类命运共同体，把世界建设得更加美好。”

This quote is a simple understanding of the universe and the laws of nature in ancient China, and contains the pursuit of values such as tolerance and open-mindedness, and harmony without uniformity in Chinese civilization. In both the speech delivered at the commemorative ceremony marking the 60th anniversary of the release of the "Five Principles of Peaceful Coexistence" on June 28, 2014 and the speech delivered at the conference marking the 200th birth anniversary of Karl Marx on May 4, 2018, President Xi Jinping quoted this saying, giving it a new meaning in the new era. He pointed out that "there are 7 billion people in the world today, over 200 countries and regions, over 2,500 ethnic groups and over 5,000 languages. Different ethnic groups and civilizations are colorful and have their own merits. Civilizations are only unique, and no one is superior to the other." "We should respect the diversity of civilizations, and promote exchanges and dialogues, peaceful and harmonious coexistence among different civilizations. We should not be self-conceited and disparage other civilizations and nations." He also pointed out that "we should look at the development trend and major problems facing the world today from the perspective of world history, adhere to the path of peaceful development, the independent foreign policy of peace, the open strategy of mutual benefit and win-win situation, constantly expand cooperation with other countries, actively participate in global governance, achieve win-win cooperation and common development in more fields and at a higher level, without relying on others or plundering others, and work together with other countries to build a community of shared future for mankind and make the world a better place."

61

海阔凭鱼跃，天高任鸟飞。

译文 Translated Text

大自然的广阔无边为鱼跃鸟飞提供了宽广的空间。

The sea is vast for the fish to leap at will; the sky is boundless for birds to fly at ease.

作者及出处 Author and Source

阮阅《诗话总龟·前集》卷三十二引《古今诗话》。

Ruan Yue, *Notes on Poets and Poetry: Anthology 1* (Vol. 32).

背景简介 Background Knowledge

阮阅（生卒年不详），北宋末期文人。

Ruan Yue (years of birth and death unknown) was a scholar in the late Northern Song Dynasty.

解析 Interpretation

阮阅《诗话总龟 · 前集》的原文是“大海从鱼跃，长空任鸟飞”，后世逐渐改编为“海阔凭鱼跃，天空任鸟飞”“海阔凭鱼跃，天高任鸟飞”等，用来比喻空间广大高阔，可以充分自由地行动，无拘无束地施展才能。2014 年 7 月 9 日，习近平主席在第六轮中美战略与经济对话和第五轮中美人文交流高层磋商联合开幕式上的致辞中便引用了这两句诗，以此表明宽广的太平洋有足够的空间容纳中美两个大国，中美双方应该加强对话，增信释疑，促进合作，确保中美关系始终不偏离构建新型大国关系的轨道。

The original lines in Ruan Yue's *Notes on Poets and Poetry: Anthology 1* were "大海从鱼跃，长空任鸟飞", and later were adapted to the modern version, which is used to mean that the space is so vast that one can move freely and show one's talents at ease. On July 9, 2014, in the speech delivered at the joint opening ceremony of the sixth round of the China-US Strategic and Economic Dialogue and the fifth round of the China-US High-Level Consultation on People-to-People Exchange, President Xi Jinping quoted these two lines as a way to express the idea that the Pacific is broad enough to accommodate both China and the United States, the two big countries, so we should strengthen dialogues, increase trust and resolve doubts, and promote cooperation, to ensure that China-US relations will never deviate from the track of building a new type of great power relationship.

二 英语名句

62

Every person, every race, every nation, has its own particular keynote which it brings to the general chord of life and of humanity. Life is not a monotone but a many-stringed harmony, and to this harmony is contributed a distinctive note by each individual.

译文 Translated Text

每一个人、每一个种族、每一个国家，都给生活和人类的总和弦带来了自己独特的基调。生活不是单调的，而是多弦的和声，每个人都为这种和声贡献了独特的音符。

作者及出处 Author and Source

安妮·贝赞特《新印度的诞生：印度事务的著作和演讲集》。

Annie Besant, *The Birth of New India: A Collection of Writings and Speeches on Indian Affairs.*

背景简介 Background Knowledge

安妮·贝赞特（1847—1933），英国社会主义者，妇女权利活动家、作家、演讲家。

Annie Besant (1847–1933) was a British socialist, female rights activist, writer and speaker.

解析 Interpretation

安妮·贝赞特赞美世界上个人、民族、国家的多样性。她认为正是这种多样性才使得全人类的生活更加美好，而尊重文化多样性也是实现世界文化繁荣的必然要求。

Annie Besant praises the diversity of individuals, nations and countries. She thinks it is this kind of diversity that makes the life of all mankind better, and the respect for cultural diversity is also inevitable for the realization of world cultural prosperity.

63

No culture can live if it attempts to be exclusive.

译文 Translated Text

如果一种文化试图排外，它就无法生存。

作者及出处 Author and Source

莫汉达斯·卡拉姆昌德·甘地《我梦想中的印度》。

Mohandas Karamchand Gandhi, *India of My Dreams*.

背景简介 Background Knowledge

莫汉达斯·卡拉姆昌德·甘地（1869—1948），印度政治家、革命家、思想家，被称为“印度国父”。

Mohandas Karamchand Gandhi (1869–1948) was an Indian statesman, revolutionary and thinker, and is referred to as “Father of the Indian Nation” .

解析 Interpretation

甘地强调文化的多样性以及跨文化交流的重要性。整个人类是一个共同体，要允许多样性思想文化的存在。甘地这句话很好地反映了包容互尊的主题，对当今世界文化的和平共处具有重要意义。

Gandhi emphasizes cultural diversity and the importance of cross-cultural communication. The whole human race is a community, which should allow the existence of diverse ideas and cultures. This quote properly reflects the theme of tolerance and mutual respect, and is of great significance to the peaceful coexistence of different cultures in today's world.

64

Exclusion is never the way forward on our shared paths to freedom and justice.

译文 Translated Text

在通往自由和公正的共同道路上，相互排斥永远不是我们前进的方向。

作者及出处 Author and Source

德斯蒙德·图图，转引自玛丽亚·林奇所著的《在非洲太阳下》。

Desmond Tutu, from *Beneath the African Sun* by Maria Lynch.

背景简介 Background Knowledge

德斯蒙德·图图，生于1931年，南非圣公会神职人员，神学家、反种族隔离活动家、人权活动家，1984年诺贝尔和平奖获得者。

Desmond Tutu (born in 1931) is a South African Anglican cleric and theologian, an anti-apartheid activist and human rights activist. Tutu was awarded the Nobel Peace Prize in 1984.

解析 Interpretation

此句出自 2010 年 3 月 12 日图图发表于《华盛顿邮报》上的《在非洲，人权状况倒退了一步》一文。他认为，任何人都不应该因其种族、性别、信仰、民族或性取向等不同，而得不到人们的爱、同情与关心。

This quote is taken from Tutu's article "In Africa, a step backward on human rights" published in *The Washington Post* on March 12, 2010. He believes that no one should be excluded from our love, compassion or concern because of their race, gender, faith, ethnicity or sexual orientation.

三 法语名句

65

Sans le respect mutuel, il n’est point de solide amitié.

译文 Translated Text

没有相互尊重，就没有牢固的友谊。

There is no firm friendship without mutual respect.

作者及出处 Author and Source

让·巴蒂斯特·布兰查《诚实人的格言》。

Jean-Baptiste Blanchard, *Maxims of the Moral People*.

背景简介 Background Knowledge

让·巴蒂斯特·布兰查（1731—1797），法国教育家。

Jean-Baptiste Blanchard (1731–1797) was a French educator.

解析 Interpretation

这句话的意思显而易见：互相尊重是友谊的基础，没有尊重就没有牢固的友谊。只有双方互相尊重，友情关系才能健康发展，才能长盛不衰。

The meaning of this quote is obvious. Mutual respect is the basis of friendship. Without respect, there will be no firm friendship. Only when both sides respect each other, can the friendship develop healthily and last forever.

66

J’ai dit l’égalité. Je n’ai pas dit l’identité.

译文 Translated Text

我是说平等，并没有说相同。

What I mean is being equal, not being identical.

作者及出处 Author and Source

维克多·雨果《九三年》。

Victor Hugo, *Ninety-Three.*

背景简介 Background Knowledge

维克多·雨果（1802—1885），法国浪漫主义作家、诗人。《九三年》是雨果创作的最后一部长篇小说。

Victor Hugo (1802–1885) was a French romantic writer and poet. *Ninety-Three* is the last novel written by Hugo.

解析 Interpretation

这句话表达了作者崇尚平等的思想——人与人之间应和而不同、平等相处。

This quote expresses the author's advocacy of equality, harmony without uniformity and equal coexistence of people.

67

La diversité des cultures humaines ne doit pas nous inviter à une observation morcelante ou morcelée. Elle est moins fonction de l'isolement des groupes que des relations qui les unissent.

译文 Translated Text

人类文化的多样性不是让我们以零散的视角去观察问题。其作用不是为了分裂，而是为了将所有人团结在一起。

The diversity of human cultures does not mean that we should observe things in fragments. It doesn' t intend to split, but to unite everyone.

作者及出处 Author and Source

克洛德·列维－斯特劳斯《种族与历史》。

Claude Lévi-Strauss, *Race and History*.

背景简介 Background Knowledge

克洛德·列维－斯特劳斯（1908—2009），法国作家、哲学家、人类学家，结构主义人类学创始人，法兰西科学院院士。

Claude Lévi-Strauss (1908–2009) was a French writer, philosopher, anthropologist, founder of structural anthropology and academician of the French Academy of Sciences.

解析 Interpretation

1952 年，联合国教科文组织出版了一系列与种族问题相关的宣传册，克洛德·列维–斯特劳斯为此写出《种族与历史》一书。在书中，作者对二十世纪四五十年代甚嚣尘上的种族主义进行了理论上的批判，同时指出：任何文化，无论多么微不足道，都是人类的共同财富，理应保留。

作者试图把进步观念与文化相对主义结合起来，强调民族文化的独特性、差异性，否认一元的文化进化观和历史进步观。他认为，任何一种文化的存在都具有合理性，没有一个标准可以绝对地评判一种文化。

In 1952, UNESCO published a series of brochures related to race, to which Claude Lévi-Strauss contributed *Race and History*. In this book, the author criticizes the theory of racism which caused a great clamor in the 1940s and 1950s, and points out that any culture, no matter how insignificant, is the common wealth of mankind and should be preserved for the sake of cultural diversity.

Claude Lévi-Strauss tries to combine the concept of progress with cultural relativism, emphasizes the uniqueness of and difference between varied national cultures, and denies the monistic concept of cultural evolution and historical progress. He thinks that the existence of any culture is reasonable, and there is no universal standard to evaluate a culture absolutely.

68

Pourquoi nous haïr? Nous sommes solidaires, emportés sur la même planète, équipage d'un même navire. Et s'il est bon que des civilisations s'opposent pour favoriser des synthèses nouvelles, il est monstrueux qu'elles se dévorent.

译文 Translated Text

为什么要相互憎恶？我们休戚与共，因为人类生存在同一个星球上，搭乘着同一艘轮船。虽然说文明对立有利于新集合的形成，但是它们相互吞噬也势必异常恐怖。

Why should we hate each other? We are in solidarity, living on the same planet, carried on the same ship. And if it is good that civilizations oppose each other to form new syntheses, it is monstrous when they devour each other.

作者及出处 Author and Source

安托万·德·圣－埃克苏佩里《人的大地》。

Antoine de Saint-Exupéry, *Terre des hommes*.

背景简介 Background Knowledge

安托万·德·圣-埃克苏佩里（1900—1944），法国作家、飞行员。

Antoine de Saint-Exupéry (1900–1944) was a French writer and pilot.

解析 Interpretation

这句话表明，作者从宇宙的角度衡量人类，告诫所属不同文明的人们不要相互憎恶，因为世界是一个整体，所有人都处在一个命运共同体中。文明在相互对抗的过程中会损失很多珍贵的东西，所以不同文明之间应该取长补短、和谐共生、共同进步，形成一个紧紧相依、休戚与共的文明大家园。

This quote shows that the author measures human beings from the specifications of the universe and warns human beings of different civilizations that they should not hate each other, because all people are in a community of shared future and the world is an integral whole. Civilizations will lose many precious things in the process of opposing each other, so various civilizations should live together in harmony, learn from others' strong points to make up for their own deficiencies, and make progress together, so as to form a home where civilizations are closely interdependent, sharing weal and woe.

69

La tolérance, c’est la civilisation par excellence.

译文 Translated Text

宽容是最杰出的文明。

Tolerance is the most preeminent civilization.

作者及出处 Author and Source

吉尔斯·佩罗，与迪迪埃·塞纳卡尔的谈话（1994 年 6 月）。

Gilles Perrault, dialogue with Didier Sénécal in June 1994.

背景简介 Background Knowledge

吉尔斯 · 佩罗，生于 1931 年，法国记者、作家、编剧。迪迪埃 · 塞纳卡尔，生于 1954 年，法国作家、译者，擅长写侦探小说。

Gilles Perrault (born in 1931) is a French journalist, writer and screenwriter. Didier Sénécal (born in 1954) is a French translator and writer who is good at writing detective stories.

解析 Interpretation

宽容是人的美德，包容是人的天性。拥有宽容才能拥有和谐，世界才会美好。

Tolerance is a human virtue and inclusiveness is human nature. Only by showing tolerance can we have harmony and can the world be beautiful.

70

Aujourd’hui, l’égalité des droits, c’est le droit pour chacun d’être différent. Celui qui opte pour la discrimination a perdu.

译文 Translated Text

如今，权利平等意味着每个人都有权不同于他人，选择歧视的人已一败涂地。

Nowadays, the equality of rights means that everyone has the right to be different from others, and those who choose to discriminate others have failed.

作者及出处 Author and Source

西蒙·佩雷斯，2016 年 3 月 30 日《费加罗报》。

Shimon Peres, in *Figaro*, March 30, 2016.

背景简介 Background Knowledge

西蒙·佩雷斯（1923—2016），于 1984 年至 1986 年任以色列总理，2007 年当选为以色列第九任总统。他致力于推动中东的和平进程，于 1994 年获得诺贝尔和平奖。

Shimon Peres (1923–2016) served as the Prime Minister of Israel from 1984 to 1986 and was elected as the 9th President of Israel in 2007. He was committed to promoting the Middle East peace process, and was awarded the Nobel Peace Prize in 1994.

解析 Interpretation

此名言旨在强调每个人都是与众不同的，世界上的人们不应存在歧视。

This quote aims to emphasize that everyone is different from others and there should be no discrimination among people in the world.

71

Sans différences, pas d’harmonie.

译文 Translated Text

没有差异，就没有和谐。

There will be no harmony without difference.

作者及出处 Author and Source

佚名。

Anonymous.

解析 Interpretation

这句话与中国的“和而不同”有着异曲同工之妙，都讲求尊重差异、求同存异、和谐共处。从辩证的角度看，长短相形，高下相倾；同样地，没有差异，和谐也便无从谈起。同时，和谐并不意味着丝毫没有差别和分歧，正相反，各美其美、美美与共的多样性之美才是真正意义上的和谐。所以说“没有差异，就没有和谐”。

This sentence is similar to China’s “harmony without uniformity”, as both stress respect for differences, seeking common ground while reserving differences, and harmonious coexistence.

From a dialectical point of view, the long and the short are shown by each other, and the high and the low depend on each other. Similarly, if there is no difference, there will be no harmony. In addition, harmony does not mean that there is no difference or divergence. On the contrary, that different kinds of beauty coexist harmoniously is a higher level of harmony. Therefore, "there will be no harmony without difference."

四 西班牙语名句

72

Toda la armonía total de este mundo está formada de discordancias.

译文 Translated Text

世界上所有的和谐都是由不同组成的。

All harmony in the world is made up of differences.

作者及出处 Author and Source

塞涅卡，“谚语格言”（Proverbia）网站。

Lucio Anneo Séneca, from the website of Proverbia.

背景简介 Background Knowledge

塞涅卡（约公元前 4—公元 65），古罗马时代著名的斯多亚派哲学家、政治家、剧作家。

Lucio Anneo Séneca (c. 4 B.C.–65 A.D.) was a famous Stoic philosopher, statesman and playwright in ancient Rome.

解析 Interpretation

塞涅卡这句话的意思是：各国、各民族都具有自己独特的文化基因，并呈现出不同的面貌，不同的文化在交流的过程中相互接纳，共同构成了绵延数千年的人类文明。在世界大家庭中，不同不应成为矛盾冲突的源头。各种看似不和谐的差异之间彼此尊重、相互包容，才能构成最大的和谐。

What Séneca means is that all countries and nations have their own unique cultural genes, showing different features, and accepting each other in the process of cultural exchange; together they constitute the human civilization that has lasted for thousands of years. In the global family, differences should not be the source of conflicts. All kinds of seemingly disharmonious differences should respect and tolerate each other; only in this way, can the greatest harmony be achieved.

73

La caridad es humillante porque se ejerce verticalmente y desde arriba; la solidaridad es horizontal e implica respeto mutuo.

译文 Translated Text

施舍是高傲的，因为它是自上而下的纵向行为；团结是横向的，是相互的尊重。

Charity is humiliating, because it is a top-down vertical behavior; solidarity is horizontal and implies mutual respect.

作者及出处 Author and Source

爱德华多·加莱亚诺，“谚语格言”（Proverbia）网站。

Eduardo Galeano, from the website of Proverbia.

背景简介 Background Knowledge

爱德华多·加莱亚诺（1940—2015），乌拉圭小说家、记者。

Eduardo Galeano (1940–2015) was a Uruguayan novelist and journalist.

解析 Interpretation

加莱亚诺这句话的意思是：同心协力是一种平等的参与，是相互尊重的表现，是人与人、国家与国家之间最重要的交往方式。

What Galeano means is that making concerted efforts is a kind of equal participation, a manifestation of mutual respect, and therefore the most important way of communication between people and between countries.

74

La diversidad de formas de vida es algo esencial (¡imagínate qué aburrimiento si faltase!) pero siempre que haya unas pautas mínimas de tolerancia entre ellas y que ciertas cuestiones reúnan los esfuerzos de todos. Si no, lo que conseguiremos es una diversidad de crímenes y no de culturas.

译文 Translated Text

生命形式的多样性是人类的一个本质特点（没有它，这个世界该会变得多么无聊！），但一定要有一些共容的基本原则，让某些问题聚集起所有的力量。若非如此，我们所能得到的将不是文化的多样，而是罪行的多样。

The diversity of life forms is an essential feature of mankind. (How boring the world would be without it!) But there must be some basic principles of tolerance, so that certain issues can gather all the strength. If not, what we can get is not the diversity of cultures, but the diversity of crimes.

作者及出处 Author and Source

费尔南多·萨瓦特尔《伦理学的邀请》。

Fernando Savater, *The Invitation of Ethics*.

背景简介 Background Knowledge

费尔南多·萨瓦特尔，生于 1947 年，西班牙哲学家。

Fernando Savater (born in 1947) is a Spanish philosopher.

解析 Interpretation

这段话的意思是：生命形式多种多样，生活方式千差万别，社会制度形色不一，不同的文化如百花一样开放在我们美丽的地球家园中。承认和尊重差异，万物和谐共生，这个世界才能真正变得丰富多彩、欣欣向荣。不同文化的差异可能会带来沟通的障碍，但如果彼此能坦诚相待，排除偏见，差异反而会成为交流的推进器，促进不同民族互相了解，取长补短，共同建构更加美好的未来。

What Savater means is that there are various forms of life, varied lifestyles, as well as different social systems, and diverse cultures are blooming like flowers on the earth, our beautiful home. Only when we recognize and respect the differences, and all things live in harmony, can the world become truly colorful and prosperous. Differences in culture may bring obstacles to communication, but if we treat each other with honesty and eliminate prejudices, differences will become the driving force that propels communication, promoting different nations to understand each other, learn from each other and build a better future together.

75

Nada nos diferencia en la esencia: ni el color de la piel, ni los credos religiosos, ni las ideologías políticas, ni las preferencias sexuales. Son apenas facetas de la rica diversidad del ser humano.

译文 Translated Text

没有什么能让我们从本质上变得不同，肤色、宗教信仰、意识形态和性取向都无法做到这一点。它们无非是人类多样性的表现而已。

Nothing can make us different in nature, neither skin color, religious belief, ideology nor sexual orientation. They are nothing but a full expression of human diversity.

作者及出处 Author and Source

胡安·曼努埃尔·桑托斯，诺贝尔奖官方网站。

Juan Manuel Santos, from the The Nobel Prize official website.

背景简介 Background Knowledge

胡安·曼努埃尔·桑托斯，生于 1951 年，于 2010 年至 2018 年任哥伦比亚总统。2016 年，因其为结束哥伦比亚内战所做的努力而获得诺贝尔和平奖。

Juan Manuel Santos (born in 1951) was the President of Colombia from 2010 to 2018. In 2016, he won the Nobel Peace Prize for his efforts to end the civil war in Colombia.

解析 Interpretation

桑托斯这几句话想说明的是：人类在肤色、宗教信仰、意识形态等方面的不同，只不过是人类多样性的反映，人类的本质是相同的，人类的共同发展并不会因为这些差异而受到影响。

What Santos means is that human differences in skin color, religious belief, ideology and so on are just a reflection of human diversity. Human nature is interlinked, and the common development of mankind will not be influenced by these differences.

第六部分

合作发展

一

汉语名句

76

一花独放不是春，百花齐放春满园。

译文 Translated Text

一种花开放，不能算是春天；百花齐放的时候，满园都是春色。

A single flower does not make a spring; when all flowers are in bloom, the garden is full of the beauty of spring.

作者及出处 Author and Source

《增广贤文》。

Enlarged Edition of Moral Texts in Former Times.

背景简介 Background Knowledge

《增广贤文》是中国明清时期的儿童启蒙读物，集结了明代以前的各种格言、谚语。

The *Enlarged Edition of Moral Texts in Former Times* is an enlightenment book for children in the Ming and Qing dynasties, which is a collection of all kinds of maxims and proverbs before the Ming Dynasty.

解析 Interpretation

2013年4月7日，习近平主席在博鳌亚洲论坛2013年年会上的主旨演讲中引用了这句话，强调各国应当在发展中兼顾彼此利益，实现共同发展。他指出："世界各国联系紧密、利益交融，要互通有无、优势互补，在追求本国利益时兼顾他国合理关切，在谋求自身发展中促进各国共同发展，不断扩大共同利益汇合点。"

In his keynote speech delivered at the Boao Forum for Asia annual conference on April 7, 2013, President Xi Jinping quoted these two lines to stress that all countries should give consideration to the mutual interests and achieve common development in the process of development. He pointed out: "All countries in the world are closely linked and their interests are blended. Therefore, they should help to supply each other's needs and complement each other's strengths. When pursuing their own interests, they should take into account the reasonable concerns of other countries; when seeking their own development, they should promote the common development of all countries and constantly enhance the convergence of common interests."

77

计利当计天下利。

译文 Translated Text

谋划利益应当谋划天下人的大利益。

The interests to be considered should be the interests of all.

作者及出处 Author and Source

于右任，转引自张良国、钱慧英编著的《名人哲理联语赏析》。

Yu Youren, from *Appreciation of Philosophical Couplets of Celebrities* by Zhang Liangguo and Qian Huiying.

背景简介 Background Knowledge

于右任（1879—1964），中国近现代政治家、教育家、书法家。“计利当计天下利”，语出于右任题写的一副对联：“计利当计天下利，求名应求万世名。”

Yu Youren (1879–1964) was a modern Chinese statesman, educator and calligrapher. “计利当计天下利” is taken from a couplet by Yu Youren, and the whole couplet goes “计利当计天下利，求

名应求万世名”, the second line of which means “the fame to be sought should be an everlasting fame”.

解析 Interpretation

于右任的联语明白晓畅，反映了儒家传统文化中轻私重公的一贯思想，勉励不应计一时、一地、一己之私，而应求全人类、全世界的“天下利”，留下可载史册的“万世名”。2013 年 10 月 3 日，习近平主席在印度尼西亚国会发表的演讲中曾引用此句，意在表明中国愿在平等互利的基础上，扩大对东盟国家开放，使自身发展更好惠及东盟国家，为世界发展谋利益。

The meaning of Yu Youren’s couplet is clear, which reflects the consistent thought of emphasizing public interests and taking private interests lightly in Confucian traditional culture, encouraging people to pursue “the interests of all” around the world instead of their own private interests at a certain time in a certain place, and to seek “an everlasting fame” which can be recorded in history. In his speech delivered at the Indonesian Parliament on October 3, 2013, President Xi Jinping quoted this line, intending to point out that China is willing to expand the scope of its opened-up areas to ASEAN countries on the basis of equality and mutual benefits, better benefit ASEAN countries with its own development and consider the interests of the whole world.

78

既以为人，己愈有；既以与人，己愈多。

译文 Translated Text

尽全力帮助他人，自己反而更加充实富有；给予他人的越多，自己得到的也就越多。

If you try your best to help others, you will become richer; the more you give others, the more you will get.

作者及出处 Author and Source

老子《老子·第八十一章》。

Lao Tzu, *Tao Te Ching* (Chapter 81).

背景简介 Background Knowledge

老子（生卒年不详），春秋时期的思想家、哲学家，道家学派的创始人和主要代表人物，曾被列为世界文化名人，世界百位历史名人之一。

Lao Tzu (years of birth and death unknown) was a thinker and philosopher in the Spring and Autumn Period. He was also the founder and main representative of the Taoist School, and has been listed as one of the world cultural celebrities and one of the world's 100 historical celebrities.

解析 Interpretation

老子认为，帮助他人和赠予他人不但不会使自己受损，反而会令自身受益，帮助、给予他人越多，自己受益就越大。这是老子朴素的辩证思想，也是中国人传承千年的价值观念和处世原则。人类是一个命运共同体，共同面临着环境污染、粮食不足、资源短缺、能源危机等全球性问题，唯有精诚合作、互帮互助才能实现共同发展。一个国家帮助其他国家越多，自己受益就越大。

Lao Tzu believes that helping others and giving to others will not make ourselves lose, but benefit ourselves instead; the more we help and give to others, the more benefits we will get. This is Lao Tzu's plain dialectical thought, and it is also the value concept and life philosophy that Chinese people have inherited for thousands of years. Today, mankind is a community of shared future, facing together global problems such as environmental pollution, food shortage, resource shortage and energy crisis. Only by sincere cooperation and mutual assistance, can we achieve common development. The more a country helps other countries, the more benefits it will get.

79

大河有水小河满，小河有水大河满。

译文 Translated Text

大河有水的话，小河的水就会充溢；小河有水的话，大河才能充盈。

When there is water in the big river, the small rivers will be filled; when there is water in the small rivers, the big river will be filled.

作者及出处 Author and Source

中国民间谚语。

Chinese proverb.

背景简介 Background Knowledge

中国古代农业文明发达，雨水、河水对农业生产十分重要，因而产生了很多相关的俗语、谚语，例如：“雨水落雨三大碗，大河小河都要满”“大河有水小河满，大河无水小河干”“大河涨水小河满”等。这里我们看到的“大河有水小河满，小河有水大河满”也一样，都体现出了中国古人的朴素智慧。

Agriculture in ancient China was rather developed. As rainwater and river water are very important to agricultural production, many related proverbs were created, such as "After three bowls of rainfall, both the big river and small river will be filled" , "If there is water in the big river, the small rivers will be full of water; if there is no water in the big river, the small rivers will be dried up" , "When the water level in the big river rises, the small rivers will be filled" and so on. The quote here is just one of them, all of which reflect the simple wisdom of the ancient Chinese people.

解析 Interpretation

这句谚语用水做比喻，形象地说明了命运与共、合作互助才能共存共赢的道理。2015 年 3 月 28 日，习近平主席在博鳌亚洲论坛 2015 年年会上的主旨演讲中指出："迈向命运共同体，必须坚持合作共赢、共同发展。东南亚朋友讲'水涨荷花高'，非洲朋友讲'独行快，众行远'，欧洲朋友讲'一棵树挡不住寒风'，中国人讲'大河有水小河满，小河有水大河满'。这些说的都是一个道理，只有合作共赢才能办大事、办好事、办长久之事。"

This proverb uses water as a metaphor to vividly illustrate the truth that only by sharing a common destiny as well as seeking cooperation and mutual assistance, can we achieve coexistence and a win-win situation. In the keynote speech delivered at the Boao Forum for Asia annual conference on March 28, 2015, President Xi Jinping pointed out that “we must adhere to win-win cooperation and common development in order to move towards a community of shared future. Our friends in Southeast Asia say that ‘the lotus flowers grow taller as the water rises’ ; our friends in Africa say ‘if you want to go fast, walk alone; and if you want to go far, walk together’ ; our friends in Europe say that ‘a single tree cannot block the chilly wind’ ; we Chinese say ‘when there is water in the big river, the small rivers will be filled; when there is water in the small rivers, the big river will be filled’ . All these sayings tell the same truth, that is, only through win-win cooperation can we do great things, good things and long-term things.”

80

孤举者难起，众行者易趋。

译文 Translated Text

一个人向上托举重物很困难，众人一起走路很容易走得快。

It's hard for a single person to lift a heavy object; it's easy to walk fast if people walk together.

作者及出处 Author and Source

魏源《默觚·治篇》。

Wei Yuan, *The Silent Goblet*: *On Governance*.

背景简介 Background Knowledge

魏源（1794—1857），清代启蒙思想家、政治家、文学家。

Wei Yuan (1794–1857) was an Enlightenment thinker, statesman and writer in the Qing Dynasty.

解析 Interpretation

这句话是说：单凭一个人的力量做事，难以取得成功；而依靠集体的力量一起行动，则事半功倍，容易取得良好的效果。2015 年 4 月 22 日，习近平主席在亚非领导人会议上发表的讲话中先后援引非洲谚语“一根原木盖不起一幢房屋”和中国的“孤举者难起，众行者易趋”，呼吁亚非国家在新形势下坚持安危与共、守望相助，把握机遇、共迎挑战。亚非国家加强互利合作，能产生“一加一大于二”的积极效应。

What this quote means is that it is difficult to succeed by relying on the strength of a single person, but it is easy to achieve good results by relying on the collective strength to act together. At the Asian-African Summit on April 22, 2015, President Xi Jinping quoted both the African proverb “One single pillar is not sufficient to build a house” and the Chinese saying “It’s hard for a single person to lift a heavy object; it’s easy to walk fast if people walk together” to appeal to Asian and African countries to adhere to the principle of sticking together through thick and thin, keeping watch and helping each other, seizing opportunities and meeting challenges together under the new situation. Promoting mutually beneficial cooperation between Asian and African countries can produce a positive effect of “one plus one makes more than two” .

81

立天下之正位，行天下之大道。

译文 Translated Text

站立在天下最光明正大的立场上，实现人类社会最远大的理想。

Stand in the right position in the world and walk on the big way under heaven.

作者及出处 Author and Source

孟子《孟子·滕文公下》。

Mencius, *Mencius* (Duke Wen of Teng, Part II).

背景简介 Background Knowledge

孟子（约公元前372—公元前289），战国时期的哲学家、思想家、政治家、教育家，是孔子之后儒家学派的代表人物，与孔子并称“孔孟”。

Mencius (c. 372 B.C.–289 B.C.) was a philosopher, thinker, statesman and educator in the Warring States Period. He was the representative of the Confucian School after Confucius, and is referred to as “Confucius and Mencius” together with Confucius.

解析 Interpretation

这是孟子关于“大丈夫”论述中的一部分。在孟子看来，“大丈夫”不仅要具备“富贵不能淫，贫贱不能移，威武不能屈”的气节，还要有“立天下之正位，行天下之大道”的理想追求。2016年1月21日，习近平主席在阿拉伯国家联盟总部发表的演讲中曾引用这句话来阐释“一带一路”倡议的初衷：中国推动大家一起加入“一带一路”朋友圈，不谋求填补“真空”，而是编织互利共赢的合作伙伴网络。“一带一路”旨在与世界其他国家分享中国机遇，使沿线国家和地区与中国一起发展，共享繁荣，促进人类共同进步。

This is a part of Mencius' discussion on “true man”. In Mencius' view, a “true man” should not only have the fine quality of “being neither corrupted by wealth, shaken by poverty, nor subdued by force”, but also need the pursuit of the ideal of “standing in the right position in the world and walking on the big way under heaven” . In the speech delivered at the Arab League Headquarters on January 21, 2016, President Xi Jinping quoted this saying to explain the original intention of China's “Belt and Road Initiative”, saying that China calls on everyone to join the “Belt and Road” circle of friends, which, instead of attempting to fill the “vacuum”, tries to build a cooperative partnership network for win-win outcomes. The “Belt and Road Initiative” aims to share China's opportunities with other countries in the world, so that the countries and regions along the “Belt and Road” will develop together with China, share prosperity and promote the common progress of mankind.

82

单则易折，众则难摧。

译文 Translated Text

一支箭容易被折断，多支箭捆在一起则难以被摧毁。

One arrow is readily broken, but many arrows bound together cannot be broken easily.

作者及出处 Author and Source

李延寿《北史·吐谷浑传》。

Li Yanshou, *History of the Northern Dynasties: Biography of Tuyuhun.*

背景简介 Background Knowledge

李延寿（生卒年不详），唐代史学家。其所著《北史》是中国“二十四史”之一，是汇合删节记载北朝历史的《魏书》《北齐书》《周书》《隋书》而编成的纪传体史书，共一百卷。

Li Yanshou (years of birth and death unknown) was a historian in the Tang Dynasty. His *History of the Northern Dynasties,* one of *The Twenty-Four Histories* in China, is a 100-volume biographical book of history compiled through a collection of abridged records of the history of the Northern Dynasties including *Book of Wei*, *Book of Northern Qi*, *Book of Zhou*, and *Book of Sui*.

解析 Interpretation

吐谷浑的首领用折箭的道理来告诫儿子们，只有兄弟齐心协力才能使国家安定稳固。今天人们时常用这个典故来强调团结的重要性。世界各国的命运紧密相连，只有各国同心协力、精诚合作，才能妥善应对各种问题和挑战。2017 年 9 月 26 日，习近平主席在国际刑警组织第八十六届全体大会开幕式上的主旨演讲中引用此句，旨在说明各国应该树立共同、综合、合作、可持续的全球安全观，通过共同努力解决人类社会发展面临的难题。

By using the principle of arrow breaking, the leader of the minority group Tuyuhun warned his sons that only with their concerted efforts could the country be stable. Nowadays, people often use this allusion to emphasize the importance of unity. The destinies of all countries in the world are closely linked; therefore, only with concerted efforts and sincere cooperation can we properly deal with various problems and challenges. In his keynote speech delivered at the opening ceremony of the 86th plenary session of the International Criminal Police Organization on September 26, 2017, President Xi Jinping quoted this saying in order to show that all countries should establish a common, comprehensive, cooperative and sustainable concept of security, and make joint efforts to solve the problems confronted by the development of human society.

83

志合者，不以山海为远。

译文 Translated Text

志同道合的人，即使被山海阻隔也不觉得遥远。

Nothing, not even mountains and oceans, can separate people with shared goals and vision.

作者及出处 Author and Source

葛洪《抱朴子·外篇·博喻》。

Ge Hong, *Pao-Pu-Tzu* (Outer Chapters).

背景简介 Background Knowledge

葛洪（约 281—341），东晋道教理论家、医药学家。

Ge Hong (c. 281–341) was a Taoist theorist and medical expert in the Eastern Jin Dynasty.

解析 Interpretation

2014 年 7 月 17 日，习近平主席在中国—拉美和加勒比国家领导人会晤上的主旨讲话中援引此句，并指出：“中国人民正在为实现中华民族伟大复兴的中国梦而奋斗，拉美和加勒比各国人民也在为实现团结协作、发展振兴的拉美梦而努力。共同的梦想和共同的追求，将中拉双方紧紧联系在一起。”虽然中拉在地理上有山海之阻，相隔万里，但只要有共同的志向和追求，彼此就不会觉得遥远。

On July 17, 2014, President Xi Jinping quoted this sentence in his keynote speech at the China-Latin America and the Caribbean Countries Leaders' Meeting and pointed out, “The Chinese people are now striving to realize the Chinese dream of the great rejuvenation of the Chinese nation. The people of Latin American and Caribbean countries are also working toward the Latin American dream of unity, coordination, development and rejuvenation. The shared dream and pursuit have brought us closely together.” Although China and Latin America are geographically separated by the breadth of the Pacific Ocean and are thousands of miles apart, we will not feel distant from each other as long as we have common aspirations and pursuits.

84

己欲立而立人，己欲达而达人。

译文 Translated Text

自己站得住，才能使别人站得住；自己发展得好，才能使别人发展得好。

To achieve success, one should let others succeed as well.

作者及出处 Author and Source

《论语·雍也》。

The Analects (Book VI, Yong Ye).

背景简介 Background Knowledge

《论语》是孔子弟子及再传弟子为记录孔子及其弟子言行而编成的语录集，较为集中地体现了孔子及儒家学派的政治主张、伦理思想、道德观念及教育原则。孔子（公元前551—公元前479），中国古代思想家、政治家、教育家，儒家学派创始人。

The Analects is a collection of quotations compiled by Confucius' disciples and his disciples' disciples to record the words and deeds of Confucius and his disciples. It embodies the political views, ethical thoughts, moral concepts and educational principles of Confucius and the Confucian School. Confucius (551 B.C.–479 B.C.) was an ancient Chinese thinker, statesman, educator, and founder of the Confucian School in the Spring and Autumn Period.

解析 Interpretation

"己欲立而立人，己欲达而达人"是孔子提出的君子立身处世的重要原则，即将心比心、推己及人，最终达到人我俱立、和谐共进的境界。2015 年 4 月 21 日，习近平主席在巴基斯坦议会发表的演讲中引用了这句话，表达中国与世界各国携手共进、互利共赢的美好愿望。人类是一个命运共同体，中国的发展不仅有利于中国，也有利于世界各国的共同发展。

This quote is an important principle for a gentleman to live in the society put forward by Confucius, that is, one should feel for others, put oneself in others' shoes, and ultimately achieve the state of common success and harmonious progress together with others. In the speech delivered at the Pakistan Parliament on April 21, 2015, President Xi Jinping quoted this remark to show that China is willing to join hands with other countries in the world and achieve a win-win situation. Mankind is a community of shared future; therefore, China's development is beneficial not only to China, but also to the common development of all countries in the world.

二 英语名句

85

Today we are faced with the preeminent fact that, if civilization is to survive, we must cultivate the science of human relationships – the ability of all peoples, of all kinds, to live together and work together in the same world, at peace.

译文 Translated Text

今天，我们面临着这样一个显而易见的事实，即文明如果还要继续存在下去，我们就必须致力于发展人际关系的科学——所有民族和所有种族在同一个世界上和睦相处、共同生活、共同发展的能力。

作者及出处 Author and Source

富兰克林·德兰诺·罗斯福，选自查尔斯·范·多伦、罗伯特·麦克亨利所著的《韦伯斯特美国历史指南：集编年的、地理的、传记的概述与汇编》。

Franklin Delano Roosevelt, from *Webster's Guide to American History: A Chronological, Geographical, and Biographical Survey and Compendium* by Charles Van Doren and Robert McHenry.

背景简介 Background Knowledge

富兰克林·德兰诺·罗斯福（1882—1945），美国第32任总统，美国历史上首位连任4届的总统，曾多次被评为美国最佳总统，被《大西洋月刊》评为影响美国的100位人物之第4名。

Franklin Delano Roosevelt (1882–1945) was the 32nd President of the United States. He was the first president in American history to serve four consecutive terms, and he was repeatedly named the best president of the United States and ranked the 4th of the 100 most influential people in American history by *The Atlantic*.

解析 Interpretation

1945年，世界反法西斯战争即将结束。在这种背景下，罗斯福总统呼吁每个人、每个国家都要学会从战争的痛苦中肩负起文明存续的使命，表达了他对世界各国和平共处、共同发展的美好愿望。

In 1945, as the war against fascism was coming to an end, President Roosevelt called on every human being and every country to learn to shoulder the mission of the survival of civilization from the agony of war, which reflects his good wishes for peaceful coexistence and common development among all countries in the world.

86

The only thing that will redeem mankind is cooperation.

译文 Translated Text

唯一可以挽救人类的就是合作。

作者及出处 Author and Source

伯特兰·罗素《伦理学和政治学中的人类社会》。

Bertrand Russell, *Human Society in Ethics and Politics*.

背景简介 Background Knowledge

伯特兰·罗素（1872—1970），英国哲学家、数学家、逻辑学家、历史学家、作家，1950年诺贝尔文学奖获得者，著名的反战人士。

Bertrand Russell (1872–1970) was a British philosopher, mathematician, logician, historian, writer and the winner of Nobel Prize in Literature in 1950. He was also an anti-war activist.

解析 Interpretation

罗素强调人类互相合作的重要性，认为世界各国必须加强合作，才能实现互利互赢、共同发展。

Russell emphasizes the importance of cooperation between human beings and believes all countries in the world need to strengthen cooperation in order to achieve mutual benefit, a win-win situation and common development.

87

Alone we can do so little; together we can do so much.

译文 Translated Text

孤掌难鸣，仅做小事；团结一致，可成大业。

作者及出处 Author and Source

海伦·凯勒，转引自约瑟夫·拉西所著的《海伦和其老师：海伦·凯勒与安妮·沙利文·梅西的故事》。

Helen Keller, from *Helen and Teacher: The Story of Helen Keller and Anne Sullivan Macy* by Joseph P. Lash.

背景简介 Background Knowledge

海伦·凯勒（1880—1968），美国现代作家、教育家、社会活动家。

Helen Keller (1880–1968) was a modern American writer, educator and social activist.

解析 Interpretation

海伦·凯勒两岁时因病致残，丧失了视觉和听觉，但在安妮老师的帮助下战胜了困境，开启了积极乐观的第二次生命。在黑暗中，她认识到一个人的力量是有限的，只有团结合作才能放大个体的价值。

Helen Keller was disabled by illness at the age of two and lost her sight and hearing unfortunately, but with the help of her teacher Anne, she overcame the adversity and started a positive and optimistic second life. Living in darkness, she realized that the power of one person is limited, and that unity and cooperation can magnify the value of individuals.

88

Cooperation is a higher moral principle than competition.

译文 Translated Text

合作是比竞争更高的道德原则。

作者及出处 Author and Source

布莱恩特·哈里森·麦吉尔《理性之声：与伟大而美好的思想革命之精神对话》。

Bryant Harrison McGill, *Voice of Reason: Speaking to the Great and Good Spirit of Revolution of Mind*.

背景简介 Background Knowledge

布莱恩特·哈里森·麦吉尔，生于 1969 年，美国作家、活动家。

Bryant Harrison McGill (born in 1969) is an American author and activist.

解析 Interpretation

在《理性之声：与伟大而美好的思想革命之精神对话》一

书中，麦吉尔探索暴力的本质，谴责人们各自为营、只关心个人利益的心态，从道德层面呼吁人们抵制恶性竞争，加强理性合作，促进共同发展。

In his book *Voice of Reason: Speaking to the Great and Good Spirit of Revolution of Mind*, McGill explores the nature of violence, and accuses people of being apt to devise good plans only for themselves and caring only about personal interests. At the moral level, he calls on people to resist vicious competition, strengthen rational cooperation and promote common development.

三 法语名句

89

Tout ce que l’homme a ajouté à l’homme, c’est que nous appelons en bloc la civilisation.

译文 Translated Text

人类之总和，我们称之为文明。

The sum of human beings is what we call civilization.

作者及出处 Author and Source

让·罗斯丹《人类——人类生物学导论》。

Jean Rostand, *Humans – Introduction to the Research of Human Biology*.

背景简介 Background Knowledge

让·罗斯丹（1894—1977），法国生物学家、作家，法兰西学院院士。他是一位自由思想者，也是一位和平主义者。

Jean Rostand (1894–1977) was a French biologist, writer,

and academician of French Academy. He was a free thinker and a pacifist as well.

解析 Interpretation

作者这句话表明的是：全人类一代又一代的技术进步共同累积和打造出了灿烂的文明，人类文明的伟大进程离不开所有人的共同努力。

What the author says shows that the brilliant civilization is accumulated and constructed by the technological progress of the whole mankind generation after generation. The great progress of human civilization is inseparable from the joint efforts of all people.

90

Notre esprit humain exige sans délai la solidarité et l'union entre les peuples et les nations au-delà des différences qui pourraient les séparer.

译文 Translated Text

人文精神是人与人之间、民族与民族之间永久的联系与团结，它超越了会导致分离的差异。

Humanistic spirit is the permanent connection and unity between people as well as between nations, which transcends the differences that may divide them.

作者及出处 Author and Source

奥古斯托·罗亚·巴斯托斯。

Augusto Roa Bastos.

背景简介 Background Knowledge

奥古斯托·罗亚·巴斯托斯（1917—2005），巴拉圭作家。他创作了许多小说和戏剧。

Augusto Roa Bastos (1917–2005) was a Paraguayan writer who wrote many novels and plays.

解析 Interpretation

作者认为人文精神是超越时间和种族的，各民族之间有跨越分歧的联系。作者说的这种人文精神，与“天下一家”的理念不谋而合。

The author thinks that the humanistic spirit transcends time and race, and there is connection between different nations, which transcends divergences. This kind of humanistic spirit the author is talking about is similar to “all people under heaven are of one family” .

91

Tout groupe humain prend sa richesse dans la communication, l'entraide et la solidarité visant à un but commun : l'épanouissement de chacun dans le respect des différences.

译文 Translated Text

人类的每个群体都在交流、互助和团结中丰富自我，以实现一个共同的目标：在尊重差异的同时实现每个群体的充分发展。

Each group of human beings enrich themselves in communication, mutual assistance and unity, so as to achieve a common goal, that is, to realize the full development of each group while respecting differences.

作者及出处 Author and Source

弗朗索瓦兹·多尔多《童年时期的几大关键阶段》。

Françoise Dolto, *The Main Stages of Childhood*.

背景简介 Background Knowledge

弗朗索瓦兹·多尔多（1908—1988），法国著名儿科学家和精神分析专家。

Françoise Dolto (1908–1988) was a famous French pediatrician and psychoanalyst.

解析 Interpretation

这句话的意思是说，人们应当尊重差异，在团结互助中互相学习、自我完善，这样才有利于每个群体充分发展、绽放自我。这符合求同存异、互帮互助的精神。

What this quote means is that people should respect differences, learn from each other and improve themselves in unity and mutual assistance, which is conducive to the full development of each group. This is in line with the spirit of seeking common ground while reserving differences and helping each other.

四
俄语名句

92

По капле дождь, а дождь реки поит: реками море стоит.

译文 Translated Text

水滴聚成雨，雨水汇成河，河流入大海。

Water drops gather into rain, rain into a river, and all rivers flow to the sea.

作者及出处 Author and Source

弗·伊·达里《俄罗斯民间谚语》。

Vladimir Ivanovich Dal, *Proverbs of the Russian People*.

背景简介 Background Knowledge

弗·伊·达里（1801—1872），俄国学者、作家、语言学家、医生，俄罗斯历史上最重要的辞书之一《现代大俄罗斯语详解辞典》的编纂者，《俄罗斯民间谚语》的作者。

Vladimir Ivanovich Dal (1801–1872) was a Russian scholar, writer, linguist and doctor. He was the compiler of the *Explanatory Dictionary of the Living Great Russian Language*, one of the most important dictionaries in Russian history, and the author of *Proverbs of the Russian People*.

解析 Interpretation

这则谚语告诉我们：一滴水的力量极其微小，但千万滴水可以汇成雨水，流入江河，最后汇聚成大海。个体的力量是很微弱的，但集体的力量却十分强大。因此，世界各国人民应齐心协力，共同发展。

This proverb tells us that the power of a water drop is extremely small, but tens of millions of water drops can gather into rain, rain into rivers, and finally flow to the sea. It reveals that individual strength is insignificant, but collective strength is very powerful. People in different countries should make concerted efforts for common development.

93

Сноп без перевясла – солома.

译文 Translated Text

拢在一起不捆的麦秸还是散麦秸。

Gathered-up wheat straw without being bundled together is still scattered wheat straw.

作者及出处 Author and Source

弗·伊·达里《俄罗斯民间谚语》。

Vladimir Ivanovich Dal, *Proverbs of the Russian People*.

背景简介 Background Knowledge

弗·伊·达里（1801—1872），俄国学者、作家、语言学家、医生，俄罗斯历史上最重要的辞书之一《现代大俄罗斯语详解辞典》的编纂者，《俄罗斯民间谚语》的作者。

Vladimir Ivanovich Dal (1801–1872) was a Russian scholar, writer, linguist and doctor. He was the compiler of the *Explanatory Dictionary of the Living Great Russian Language*, one of the most important dictionaries in Russian history, and the author of *Proverbs of the Russian People*.

解析 Interpretation

这条谚语以麦秸为喻，生动形象地说明了这样一个道理：人类要建设一个共同繁荣的世界，就应该团结一致、协同进步，而不应该以邻为壑、画地为牢。

With wheat straw as a metaphor, this proverb vividly illustrates such a truth, that is, if human beings want to build a world of common prosperity, we should be united and make concerted progress, instead of seeking our own interests at the expense of the neighboring countries and restricting our activities to a designated area.

94

Общественный прогресс истинный – в большем и большем единении людей.

译文 Translated Text

社会真正的进步，在于人类越来越紧密的团结。

The real progress of society lies in the increasingly close unity of mankind.

作者及出处 Author and Source

列夫·尼古拉耶维奇·托尔斯泰《列·尼·托尔斯泰二十二卷作品集》。

Lev Nikolayevich Tolstoy, *Collected Works of Lev Nikolayevich Tolstoy in Twenty-two Volumes* (Selected Diaries).

背景简介 Background Knowledge

列夫·尼古拉耶维奇·托尔斯泰（1828—1910），俄国批判现实主义作家、思想家、哲学家。

Lev Nikolayevich Tolstoy (1828–1910) was a Russian critical realist writer, thinker, and philosopher.

解析 Interpretation

托尔斯泰在此处强调了全人类团结一致的重要性。在托尔斯泰看来，人类应抛弃利己主义，齐心协力追求共同福祉。每个国家、每个民族的前途命运都休戚与共、紧密相连，居住在同一个地球上的人类是一个和睦团结的大家庭，应该同舟共济，共同推动全人类的发展进步。

In this remark, Tolstoy emphasizes the importance of the unity of all mankind. In Tolstoy's view, we should abandon egoism and make concerted efforts to pursue the common well-being of all mankind. The future and destiny of every country and every nation are closely linked, sharing weal and woe. Human beings living on the same planet should be united and work together to build a harmonious and united family, and jointly facilitate the development and progress of all mankind.

95

И лес шумит дружней, когда деревьев много.

译文 Translated Text

树木多的时候，连森林的响声都是和谐的。

When there are many trees, the sound of the forest is more concordant and harmonious.

作者及出处 Author and Source

阿·尼·桑扎罗夫斯基《美丽的大自然》。

A. N. Sanzharovsky, *Beautiful Nature*.

背景简介 Background Knowledge

阿·尼·桑扎罗夫斯基，生于1938年，俄罗斯作家，其著作《美丽的大自然》中收录了大量关于自然的谚语。

A. N. Sanzharovsky (born in 1938) is a Russian writer whose book *Beautiful Nature* contains a large number of proverbs about nature.

解析 Interpretation

这是大自然教会人们的哲理。作者喜爱森林，他认为：众多的树木生长在一起时，才能形成森林；当风掠过树叶时，树木共同发出的声响才和谐悦耳。人如同树木，形成集体后才能发挥出更大的优势。

This is a philosophy that nature teaches people. The author especially loves the forests in nature and he thinks that only when a large number of trees grow together can a forest be formed and that when the wind sweeps past the leaves, the sound is harmonious and pleasant to the ear. People are just like trees and they will have more advantages when they form a collective.

五 西班牙语名句

96

Un dedo no hace mano, pero sí con sus hermanos.

译文 Translated Text

一指不成手，五指有合力。

One finger does not make a hand, and five fingers form a joint force.

作者及出处 Author and Source

佚名，选自西班牙在线教育平台“初等教育天地”（Mundo Primaria）整理的谚语集锦。

Anonymous, from the collection of proverbs sorted out by the website of Mundo Primaria (The World of Primary Education), which is a Spanish online educational platform.

解析 Interpretation

这句谚语是说，人与人之间应像一个手掌上的五根手指一样紧密团结、互信互助。只有以团结取代分歧、以理性消除偏见，才能凝聚起最大合力，战胜共同的困难，谋求共同的利益，促进共同的发展。

What this proverb means is that people should be as close and united as the five fingers of a hand, with mutual trust and mutual assistance. Only by replacing divergences with unity and eliminating prejudices using rationality, can we gather the greatest strength, overcome common difficulties, seek common interests and promote common development.

六
阿拉伯语名句

97

النوع الإنساني لا يتم وجوده إلا بالتعاون.

译文 Translated Text

人类的本质仅在于合作。

The essence of human beings lies only in cooperation.

作者及出处 Author and Source

伊本·赫勒敦（ابن خلدون）。

Ibn Khaldūn.

背景简介 Background Knowledge

伊本·赫勒敦（1332—1406），中世纪阿拉伯哲学家、历史学家、社会学家。

Ibn Khaldūn (1332–1406) was an Arab philosopher, historian and sociologist in the Middle Ages.

解析 Interpretation

这句话表明，大到世界各民族，小到社会各团体，只有相互合作、互帮互助，才能延续生命、繁衍不息。

This quote shows that only by promoting and helping each other can the world's ethnic groups and social groups continue to this day and keep flourishing.

98

السير بوحده سريع، والسير مع الجماعة بعيد.

译文 Translated Text

独行快，众行远。

He who travels alone goes fast, but he who travels in company goes far.

作者及出处 Author and Source

阿拉伯谚语。

Arab proverb.

背景简介 Background Knowledge

2016 年 1 月 19 日，习近平主席在埃及《金字塔报》发表的题为《让中阿友谊如尼罗河水奔涌向前》的署名文章中引用了这句谚语。

On January 19, 2016, President Xi Jinping quoted this Arab proverb in the signed article entitled “Let China-Arab Friendship Surge Forward Like the Nile” in the Egyptian newspaper *Al-Ahram*.

解析 Interpretation

这句谚语体现了人与人之间、国与国之间合作共赢的协作理念。在当今复杂多变的国际形势下，世界各国应始终秉持团结合作的精神，只有这样，路才能越走越宽、越走越远。

This proverb shows the concept of “win-win cooperation” between people as well as between countries. In today’s complicated and rapidly changing international context, only by always upholding the spirit of unity and cooperation can all countries in the world blaze broader and longer paths forward.

99

حمل الجماعة خفيف.

译文 Translated Text

众擎易举。

Many hands make light work.

作者及出处 Author and Source

杨言洪主编《阿拉伯语汉语成语谚语辞典》。

A Dictionary of Arabic and Chinese Idioms and Proverbs, Ed. Yang Yanhong.

解析 Interpretation

该句原意为“众人负重，轻而易举”，指众人齐心协力时，无论多么重的东西都能够轻易地举起来，引申为“众擎易举”。该句意在说明，无论是个人还是国家，都不应该忽视合作的巨大力量，应通过互相合作、群策群力的方式来谋求共同发展。

This proverb means that when people make concerted efforts, no matter how heavy things are, they can be easily lifted. It is intended to show that neither individuals nor countries should ignore the great power of cooperation, and they should seek common development through mutual cooperation, collective wisdom and concerted efforts.

100

أضئ لي أقدح لك.

译文 Translated Text

你为我照明，我为你打火。

You hold a lamp for me and I carry a torch for you.

作者及出处 Author and Source

杨言洪主编《阿拉伯语汉语成语谚语辞典》。

A Dictionary of Arabic and Chinese Idioms and Proverbs, Ed. Yang Yanhong.

解析 Interpretation

此谚语强调了合作共赢的理念：人与人之间、国与国之间应当加强合作，互相帮扶，这样才能为双方的发展注入源源不断的动力。

This proverb emphasizes the concept of “win-win cooperation”, that is, people and countries alike should strengthen cooperation and help each other, so as to inject continuous driving force into the development of both sides.